The Business of Science

The Business of Science

The risks and rewards of research and development

DAVID FISHLOCK

Associated Business Programmes
London

English Language Edition, except USA, published by
Associated Business Programmes Ltd
17 Buckingham Gate, London SW1

Published in the USA by
Halsted Press, a Division
of John Wiley & Sons Inc.
New York

First published 1975

This book has been printed in Great Britain by
The Anchor Press Ltd, Tiptree, Essex, and bound by
W. J. Rawlinson (Bookbinders) Ltd of London

ISBN 0 85227 031 3

To my son, Bill

Contents

Introduction

Early in 1973 the publishers invited me to write a book about the Concorde project, the most ambitious technological venture in the history of Britain. What they sought was neither a 'wonders of modern aviation' approach nor a book that tried to show how misbegotten was the whole project. They sought an appraisal of Concorde as a series of Government decisions, from the original Anglo-French alliance of 1962, through the crisis of 1965 when it so nearly was axed as an economy measure, to the maiden flight in 1969 and the bitter debate ever since because orders stubbornly refused to flow.

I turned down the proposal because I do not believe that Concorde, whatever its eventual fate, is representative of Britain's performance in handling high technology ventures. By this I mean ventures which attempt to harness science and engineering at fairly profound levels to some new commercial or national objective. Concorde is representative in so far as it shows yet again that Britain is capable of considerable technical achievements. Where Concorde is not representative is in the underlying motives of government—both in Britain and France—in supporting the project through a dozen years of unprecedented inflation in development costs. The primary motive, in contrast to what apologists and critics alike seem to believe, has never been an unshakable faith that some day the project would pay off in any commercial sense. The primary motive has always been to keep fully stretched and prepared some of Europe's most powerful defence contractors. For Britain and France, Concorde is part of the price of national security. Provided the two nations do not embark on large production runs of unsaleable and uneconomic aircraft, it is not even a particularly large price to have paid for the purpose it has served.

Britain, since the Second World War, has indulged in a great many ventures in high technology often, although by no means always, at the state's expense. Some have succeeded—outstanding examples include float glass, a private industry venture, cephalosporin and nuclear submarines, both joint government–industry projects, and nuclear fuel, wholly a state venture. Some have failed and been heard of no more, such as Ardil, ICI's attempt to market synthetic wool, and the Rotodyne, Fairey's project for a vertical-take-off seventy-passenger aircraft from which the government withdrew its support in 1962. Of both, well-informed people have said that 'it never looked like the real thing'. Still others have been technical successes yet failed to impress others, or impress quickly enough to find a commercial niche. By the early 1970s increases in the price of coal and oil were making Britain's investment in magnox nuclear power stations in the 1950s, originally quite uneconomic, look very attractive indeed. The cheapest electricity from a modern station was being put out by a magnox station. But the world had moved on—much higher interest rates made it unattractive to build more of these stations.

Decisions on whether to go forward or to abandon projects, which way to turn at decisive points in such projects, are rarely easy, rarely as clear-cut as their advocates—and the Press—are inclined to pretend. Great skill and care may be needed to demonstrate firmly yet diplomatically to cabinet ministers or Congressional committees, as well as to boards of directors, that a telephone or transport system or a nuclear reactor that seems merely to be second-best—slower, clumsier, even obsolescent—will in fact be the best in a certain situation. The proof may invoke factors as unquantifiable as native skills and traditions, security of the system and perhaps of supplies, even public apprehension. Too often, the importance of such factors are underestimated or ignored by reporters fired with enthusiasm for the straightforward technological or economic 'best buy'.

My counter-proposal was for a book that examined a variety of high technology projects, mostly in Britain, but drawing upon events overseas—in the United States especially—where they seemed relevant to Britain's experience. Its purpose would be to show that post-war British experience, despite its numerous costly failures, contained some solid successes and some valuable lessons which, if consistently followed, should ensure a much higher rate of success in the future. In short, it would attempt to show how to make a success of the business of science. How far, on the basis of this appraisal, I think we can go towards writing a specification for success in such projects I have tried to show in my final chapter.

As science editor of the *Financial Times* for the last seven years I have had unrivalled opportunities to examine, appraise and report upon a great variety of projects and programmes in Britain, the United States and a dozen other countries. In writing this book I have drawn freely upon my reports and notes, as well as views expressed publicly and in private by many men of science and business who have thought deeply about the problems of managing high technology projects. Wherever I felt free to disclose my source I have done so gratefully. But I am nonetheless very grateful to the many more who must go unacknowledged in a short text; and also those who were kind enough to read and comment on parts of the text in manuscript, among them Sir Brian Flowers, Sir Robert Cockburn, Sir Alastair Pilkington, Dr. Walter Marshall, Mr. J. V. L. Parry and Mr. B. T. Price. Any errors of fact or misjudgments, of course, remain my own responsibility.

David Fishlock
Jordans,
February 1974.

CHAPTER 1

Where are they now?

'. . . I heard an eminent colleague declare at a congress: "The results that I reported last year were based on facts that are no longer available"—a form of recantation that should have delighted Galilei without offending the Inquisition.'

Prof. Erwin Chargaff, writing in *Nature*, 1974

Ask people for an example of a great all-British invention of recent times and the chances are good that they will say the hovercraft. Ask people for an example of a great British inventor of modern times and the chances are nearly as high that they will say Sir Christopher Cockerell, the bristly inventor of the hovercraft, for which he was knighted in 1969. 'An important moment in history— the birth of a new era in transport' is how the public début of the hovercraft is described in a book published as recently as 1970 to commemorate the coming-of-age of the National Research Development Corporation. The NRDC is the government agency set up by the post-war Labour government as the patron of British invention. The book quotes its author's own Press cuttings of the previous ten years in claiming that 'Cockerell's invention is going to be one of this country's biggest money-spinners of all times.'[1]

The grandly-styled British Hovercraft Corporation was set up as a consortium owned 65 per cent by Westland Aircraft, 25 per cent by Vickers and 10 per cent by NRDC. Its purpose was to design and build hovercraft to cross almost any terrain. But even by 1970 its commercial record fell short of the brave forecasts of a decade before: only about fifty hovercraft sold, and only four of them sizeable ferries. One more of the big Mountbatten-class SRN–4 ferries has been built since. Commercially speaking the new British money spinner has taken an unconscionable long time to get off the ground. A report from the Programmes Analysis Unit in 1971 forecast sales of only £90 million for both hovercraft and hydrofoils by 1986.[2] The hovercraft failed to feature among the top ten NRDC inventions in earnings in 1972–3; a list which included dental cement and an

[1] Peter Fairley, *Project X*, Mayflower Paperback, 1970, p. 90.
[2] The *Financial Times*, 27 September 1971.

anti-coagulant extracted from snake venom. By 1974 NRDC had invested about £3 million of public money in hovercraft. Returns amounted to only about £1 million. If the Corporation were backing the air-cushion principle today, Bill Makinson, its chief executive, told me early in 1974, it would be putting the emphasis on its industrial uses rather than on a revolutionary method of transport.

The hovercraft is no isolated example of a British invention that is failing to live up to commercial expectations.

How much longer must we wait [asked the renowned Oxford economist Professor John Jewkes in his Wincott Memorial lecture in 1972] for efficient battery-operated motor cars which will enable the pounding, smelly reciprocating engine to be thrown on the scrapheap; or the typewriter which will type as one dictates, which will release hundreds of thousands of young women for other more interesting tasks; or the audiovisual cassettes which will enable us to break away from the tyranny and the interminable boredom of modern television; or a cure for the common cold; or much cheaper and efficient ways of digging tunnels so that the surface of the earth could be re-occupied by the people instead of being over-run by machines; or really substantial cuts in the costs of desalination rendering it possible to turn deserts into gardens?[1]

Jewkes' list can be easily extended. Where is the fuel cell that NRDC was persuaded to back with public funds as a simple and highly efficient way of converting a liquid or gaseous fuel directly into electricity? Where is the air-cushioned hovertrain that was going to carry its passengers on vibration-free journeys at speeds of several hundred miles an hour?

Where is the Collins robot miner that was going to permit the National Coal Board to win coal automatically from seams too thin and inaccessible for man to work?

Where is nuclear fusion, the tamed thermonuclear weapon, that would solve all further problems of energy supplies?

Where is carbon fibre, the slender filaments of pure carbon of which I once wrote blithely: 'Each [RB.211] engine will need some hundreds of pounds of carbon fibre. The alternative, titanium, fabricated for the very high stresses these blades will encounter, would lead to an engine appreciably heavier, noisier and less efficient.'[2] Nevertheless the RB.211 engines are using titanium for blades, not carbon fibre.

[1] John Jewkes, *Government and High Technology*, Occasional Paper 37, Institute of Economic Affairs, 1972.
[2] David Fishlock, 'Bright future for fibres', *New Scientist*, 15 May 1969, p. 12.

Private ventures

Each of those lines of progress was being pursued with public cash. Is it true, as Jewkes asserts, that 'with private effort the glitter of all things bright and beautiful is toned down by the shadow of the balance sheet and the possibility of bankruptcy'? Is private industry immune from the mistakes of government in managing high technology? Where is the cure for cancer so confidently anticipated in the mid-1960s by the research-conscious drug companies no less than by the charity- and state-funded cancer research establishments? Where is the 200 h.p. T8 gas-turbine motor car that Rover first rolled out back in 1950? Where are the plastic bricks into which Guinness plunged its cash in the late 1960s? Whatever became of the video-telephone? Flat-screen TV seems no nearer now than when electrical manufacturers first boasted of this goal back in the 1950s. Whatever happened to ICI's efforts to make artificial wool; and Hawker Siddeley's attempts to sell a much more advanced locomotive called Kestrel? Whatever happened to all those brave plans for computerised robots that would take the grinding boredom and labour from factory work by automatically cutting the metal, handling the parts in uncongenial conditions, and finally assembling them into finished products? All these highly publicised quests were private ventures. Again the list could be extended without difficulty.

The 1950s and 1960s were salad days for scientists and inventors in Britain. Never before had they stood so high in public esteem, courted and fêted as the men who could find the answers to affluent society's ills: cures for the latterday killers like coronaries and cancer; treatments for less lethal but highly distressing diseases, such as arthritis, and also for industry's adverse effects, such as pollution and mine deaths; ways of avoiding the tedium and toil of office and factory work. Throughout the land, research budgets were burgeoning. Industrial research directors were scouring the countryside of Berkshire and Buckinghamshire for elegant houses that they could turn into research centres set in pastoral surroundings, conducive to original thinking and far from the pressures of factory-floor problems. New patrons of science like the NRDC and the merchant bankers were searching the land for ideas and inventions that industry might have missed, into which they could invest their cash.

At the same time the government and its agencies were starting big new research centres: the atomic energy laboratories at Risley, Lancashire, at Dounreay in the north of Scotland, and at Winfrith in Dorset; the National Engineering Laboratory near Glasgow, and Warren Springs at Stevenage for mineral and chemical treatments; the several new research centres of the Central Electricity Generating Board. (The latter even included its own big nuclear laboratory devoted to problems of nuclear stations once they were built. No consideration seems to have been given to the idea that this was a role the existing atomic establishments might be well-equipped to take on, as their task of developing a given nuclear system drew to an end.)

The new government laboratories, and older but still growing laboratories like the Royal Aircraft Establishment at Farnborough (Europe's biggest research centre today) had one basic mission: to hasten the processes of invention and discovery. It was a concept born of wartime experience in such fields as atomic energy, gas turbines, radar, new drugs and the techniques of chemical warfare. In all these cases it was shown that a crash programme could greatly accelerate progress. Thus was born the idea that, given enough cash and encouragement, scientists could solve *any* problem, from a cure for cancer to a cure for a cold. Understandably enough, the scientist himself did little at this time to discourage the idea.

Publicising science

All this was abetted by another phenomenon of the mid- to late 1950s, a blossoming of the craft of science writing in Britain. Until then the regular science correspondent, describing and commenting on the progress and financing of research and development, wrote mostly for the more serious newspapers. Suddenly the popular national papers, provincial papers and magazines awoke to the fact that the doings of science were highly newsworthy topics. What clinched the matter for most British editors was the launching of the first national nuclear energy programme in 1955, followed closely by the royal opening of Calder Hall, the world's first large nuclear steam supply system for electric power generation, in 1956; and the launch by Russia of Sputnik, the world's first artificial satellite in 1957.

A study by Davies and Sklair of coverage of science and technology by four British newspapers—*The Times*, the *Daily Express*, the *Daily Mirror* and the London *Evening Standard*—shows that in absolute terms it has expanded substantially over the twenty years 1949–69—although in relation to the overall increase in news coverage, however, the increase is really quite small.[1] *Table 1*, based on a study of Press reports for the month of February in the years 1949, 1959 and 1969, shows the change in coverage both absolutely and as a percentage of the total paper.

[1] Leslie Sklair, *Organised Knowledge*, Hart-Davis MacGibbon, 1973, p. 201.

Table 1 Change in science coverage in the British Press, 1949–69

	Feb. 1949		Feb. 1959		Feb. 1969	
	Total*	%	Total	%	Total	%
Daily Express	262	1·24	550	0·95	783	1·21
Daily Mirror	237	0·65	469	0·86	913	1·46
Evening Standard	197	0·91	330	0·85	615	0·81
The Times	314	0·83	1,089	1·49	3,327	2·95

* Column-inches

Among the scientific events of the mid-1950s was the debut late in 1956 of a new journal. The *New Scientist*, as its founder-editor Percy Cudlipp (who a few years before had been one of the most eminent of national newspaper editors) once wrote, was to be a link between science and industry. It would report technological innovations and promising lines of research. It would pay careful attention to the scientifically progressive sections of industry and would help, by describing their activities, to create a growing interest in scientific applications among industry as a whole.

In the early years its highly authoritative explanations of every facet of technology and science, written wherever possible by the foremost practitioner in a particular field yet painstakingly edited for assimilation by the non-expert, were eagerly seized upon by other writers as well as by scientists anxious to keep abreast of progress elsewhere in science, if only to see that their own interests were not being neglected in the gold rush.

Lest I leave the impression that *New Scientist* editors hung on to every word and each prediction of the wise men of science and engineering, let me hasten to say that by the start of the 1960s the journal was making its own critical appraisals of projects and plans. Increasingly it was finding flaws in the proposals for harnessing science. In short it was attempting what later became dignified by the expression 'technology assessment'.

In 1964, for example, it ran a critique of an ambitious scheme proposed by Westland Aircraft, an NRDC licensee of hovercraft patents and principal industrial sponsor of the hovercraft, for a cross-Channel ferry service based on a fleet of a new 150-ton craft, the SRN-4, still on the drawing board. The scheme's main conclusion was that a fairly modest fleet of these hovercraft could be expected to cope adequately with the anticipated growth in cross-Channel traffic for the next twenty years or so, and that the service it proposed would make a handsome profit. It invited investment of

£34 million in capital costs (mostly in upwards of sixteen hovercraft) and anticipated the need for another £106 million a year in running costs to establish a service it estimated would earn £192 million a year.

The flaw in the scheme seemed to lie in the fact that the traffic on the proposed Dover–Calais route is extremely peaky and the route is too short to warrant the heavy investment proposed. Forecasts of car traffic for 1985 indicated that for all but a few days in August, when all sixteen hovercraft would be fully occupied, the demand could be met by less than eight craft. In midwinter a single craft would suffice. The scheme, in short, was designed for the financial benefit of a hovercraft manufacturer rather than a transport operator. As Dr. Sydney Jones, research and development chief at British Rail, points out bluntly, anyone who does not believe such a scheme is a nonsense commercially 'should work out the return on that capital employed to finance the purchase of that half of the fleet used only for a few days in August'.

When, a few months after this critique was published, I asked Richard Stanton-Jones, Cockerell's brilliant chief designer and the main architect of the scheme, what progress was being made, he ruefully admitted, 'none'. Every time they had raised the topic with a potential sponsor, he said, they had been challenged with the critique and the questions it raised. To this day, a decade on, those questions have never been answered. Five SRN–4s are plying the English Channel but by 1973 no service had made a profit. The indications are that the hovercraft needs an entirely new propulsion system—a major development project—before it will emerge as a commercially viable proposition.

Slowly, as the 'sixties advanced, it dawned on those who administered science that there was a basic fallacy in the idea that big research centres and crash programmes would hasten the pace of scientific understanding and discovery. What the experiences of the Second World War had shown was simply that the pressures (and financial freedom) of crash programmes could hasten the *application* of discoveries. The basic discoveries that led to the great technical advances of the Second World War—atomic energy, rockets, jet engines, new drugs, radar, nerve gases, and so on—had all been made before the war, in some cases long before. The big post-war boom in national laboratories had done little or nothing to hustle science along. At best it had hustled development and application along. If an understanding of the basic scientific principles involved was still missing, and there was no general agreement which way to start looking—as is the case, the experts seem to agree, with cancer research at the moment—crash programmes were highly unlikely to yield any favourable result.

How the white heat cooled

Long before the end of its six years of office the Labour government of 1964–70 had begun to tighten the purse-strings of science and technology. The white heat of scientific revolution, as Harold Wilson had enthused in 1963, may have helped his government to regain office; but if he ever had any illusions that science and technology might be harnessed again, as it had in the Second World War, to help win a quick victory in the economic battles Britain was fighting, he soon changed his mind. The lead-time and the cost of harnessing science were far too great to yield quick results in terms of the trade balance or to discourage the world-wide enthusiasm at that time for selling sterling.

At first glance the Labour government's dominant influence on the British research and development budget was a rather negative one. The public sector of research finance was dominated at the 'basic' end of the spectrum by high-energy physics and at the 'project' end by aircraft, weapons, space and nuclear energy. Altogether, the public sector accounted for some £450 million (58·4 per cent) of the £771 million spent on research and development in 1964–5.

Just six months after Labour took office it killed the TSR.2, the most advanced warplane under development at the time outside of the us and Russia. Another major aviation project was also abruptly ended, the P.1154, a supersonic version of the 'jump-jet' with its new BS.100 engine. Also terminated were studies of the jumbo-sized Belfast military freighter, and the HS.681 vertical take-off transport. The Concorde project, still less than three years old, was spared, not because the new government was convinced of its economic merits but simply because it could not untangle the Anglo-French development contract at an acceptable cost. But the Labour government terminated Farnborough studies of a very much faster airliner, for hypersonic flight, using the so-called 'wave-rider' concept; and parallel work by Bristol Siddeley on the ramjet as its potential power plant.

In 1967 a nuclear research programme, in which only eight years before Britain was claiming to lead the world, was severely curtailed. The government announced that funds for controlled thermonuclear fusion, then about £5 million a year, were to be halved over the course of the following five years. Later that year the state-owned Central Electricity Generating Board abruptly abandoned, unfinished, a £2 million experiment in MHD (magnetohydrodynamics), an adventurous energy concept. The decision, taken because the concept of an MHD 'topper' squeezing extra efficiency from a fossil power station was no longer economically so attractive, caused consternation in university circles where funds for all related research in high-temperature combustion were also abruptly ended. In 1968 came news that the government was rejecting the advice of its own scientific counsellors and refusing to join the other twelve member nations of CERN, the European Organisation for Nuclear Research in Geneva, in building a big new 'atom-smasher' of 300 GeV. Talk at that time was of a machine that would cost at least £180 million. In 1970, shortly before leaving office, the government withdrew from ELDO, the European Launcher Development Organisation in Brussels, which was trying to build a European rocket capability for satellite launches.

Each of these decisions could be justified individually. Least justified, perhaps, was the cutback in fusion funds where there are reasons for thinking that personality differences among the scientific advisers involved contributed to a decision ostensibly based on the chaotic state of nuclear fusion physics in 1967. The CERN decision, on the other hand, actually led to a much sounder and much cheaper scheme for a still more powerful machine of 400 GeV; a scheme, now well under way, to which Britain itself made a major contribution. But mostly they were sensible decisions, necessary initial steps towards a tighter control of the national research effort.

Viewed as a whole, however, the Labour government's record scarcely seems to add up to a conviction that Britain's salvation lay in science—or at least not along the paths the technologists were treading in the 1960s. Neither was the Labour government particularly conspicuous in promoting major new research and development projects of its own. It firmly rejected two fairly popular schemes— for a national programme on undersea engineering and exploration, and for an experimental nuclear-powered ship. It also turned down the idea of developing at public expense a novel type of gas turbine, driven by hot helium gas, that could mate with an advanced nuclear steam supply system called the high-temperature reactor. The Germans who had hoped that such a gas turbine might be developed collaboratively were told by Britain's Minister of Technology, Mr. Anthony Wedgwood Benn, that it was no part of his brief to provide more competition for Britain's ailing steam turbine industry.

Yet Britain's research budget had continued to grow (*see figure 1*). In 1969–70 the total spent was £1,082 million, of which the public sector (government, state-owned industries and universities) provided £617 million (57 per cent). Research is a highly labour-intensive activity but, as the chart shows, the national research budget during the mid-1960s was outpacing inflation.

The decision was taken early in Labour's regime to launch Britain's second nuclear power programme, calling for up to 8,000

MW of power from advanced gas-cooled reactors (AGRs), a technology developed over the previous ten years. Two modest projects were also begun to explore new methods of high-speed surface transport: British Rail's advanced passenger train (APT) and the hovertrain, each for an initial outlay of £2 million. The APT project was a success

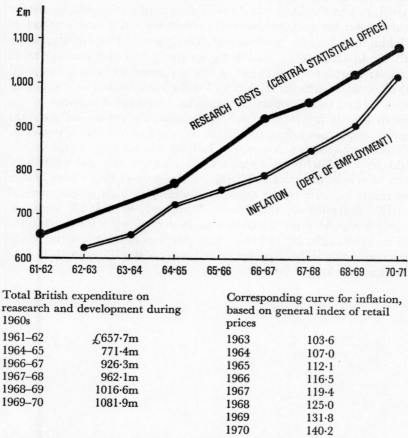

Total British expenditure on research and development during 1960s		Corresponding curve for inflation, based on general index of retail prices	
1961–62	£657·7m	1963	103·6
1964–65	771·4m	1964	107·0
1966–67	926·3m	1965	112·1
1967–68	962·1m	1966	116·5
1968–69	1016·6m	1967	119·4
1969–70	1081·9m	1968	125·0
		1969	131·8
		1970	140·2

Figure 1 Rise of research costs *v.* rise of inflation during the 1960s.

and is the transport technology on which British Rail's long-term strategy is founded. The hovertrain project was abandoned in 1973, when expenditure had reached £5 million (£2 million had been the initial estimate to reach this stage) and the project was poised for an expensive leap forward, yet there was not the slightest sign of any potential market. In a different sector of transport the Labour government offered an unusually high level of support, 70 per cent, for a Rolls-Royce private venture, the RB.211 aero-engine for Lockheed. It also authorised the prototype fast reactor.

A big decision

One major decision to launch a new civil project was that taken in 1968, to join the Dutch and the Germans in a tripartite treaty for the development and commercial exploitation of a new method of enriching uranium for nuclear fuel. The gas centrifuge treaty, as we shall see in chapter 11, was both a courageous and an inevitable decision: courageous, because of the awesome technical, financial and diplomatic difficulties that had to be surmounted in competing with a virtual US monopoly on uranium enrichment supplies to the western world; inevitable, because Britain, for reasons of national security, could not afford to entrust its supplies of nuclear power as well as oil to a foreign power. But Labour was well aware that there could be no short-term returns from its tripartite gas centrifuge treaty. Even in terms of publicity for the project there were severe constraints because of the secrecy—military as well as commercial security—surrounding the details. Moreover, even if all went extremely well, the project would remain very hungry for funds until well into the 1980s. By 1985 the three partners in the tripartite 'club' expect to make an investment of at least £500 million in their new uranium enrichment process.

CHAPTER 2

Is it worth it?

'The relationship between research and prosperity [is] as predictable as that between prayer and deliverance . . .'

Dan Greenberg, *Science and Government Report*, 1973

At Scarborough in October 1963 in Mr. Harold Wilson's famous 'Statement on Science', the Labour Party leader sounded a clarion call for the country to harness 'science to society and society to science'. In a speech that may well have helped him to power the following year, he spoke of 'the Britain that is going to be forged in the white heat of this revolution . . .'

Science and its achievements did not figure strongly in the Labour government's defence of its record as the election of 1970 approached. No one should have been very surprised. Several major technological projects by that time were looking far from sanguine. The second nuclear programme was deep in trouble, with Dungeness B, the first of the new power stations to be ordered, still as far in time from completion as when the order was placed in 1966. As fast as the formidable technical problems of Concorde were being solved fresh ones were raised by the public's new-found enthusiasm for showing concern about the environment. And then there was Rolls-Royce. The biggest export contract Britain had ever landed, for RB.211 engines for the Lockheed Tristar, was beginning to look like a Pyrrhic victory for the nation as it became clear that once again the aircraft industry had seriously under-estimated its research and development costs.

Where Labour's policies for harnessing science were beginning to bite—in uranium enrichment and machine tool development, in computer technology and in re-orientating the efforts of the national laboratories—the results were still too remote from the market to yield any capital politically. National programmes to improve lubrication or reduce maintenance costs might be important economically but they had little allure for the voter.

John Duckworth, chief executive of the National Research Development Corporation throughout the 'sixties, tells a story that sums up well the prevailing view of science as the solution to Britain's economic troubles. Duckworth was being considered by a leading

City merchant bank, N. M. Rothschild, for a post in which he would take charge of the venture capital or riskier end of the business. Over lunch with the bankers the chairman began brightly: 'Tell us, Mr. Duckworth, if we gave you £1 million how would you invest it?' 'In property,' came the prompt reply, and Duckworth was given the job.

High technology

One man who, as we saw in the previous chapter, is in no doubt at all that governments at least should steer clear of support for high technology is Professor John Jewkes. Although an economist, Jewkes is no stranger to the business of science. He is senior author of an important essay, first published in 1958, on innovation and how it comes about.[1] In his Wincott Memorial Lecture in 1972 Jewkes concluded that what a government at any one time should undertake ought to be determined by what it has already undertaken and how well it is carrying out these self-appointed tasks.

> If our present-day governments would avow the falling standards of success in their primary jobs and decide that activities with lower priorities should be dropped, surely involvement in civil high technology should be regarded as one of the first for the discard. For here the aims of governments seem uncertain, the charting of the original course a most baffling task, and the procedures for controlling the subsequent course highly obscure.[2]

Jewkes bases his case on three sectors of technology in particular: atomic energy, where reactor development has cost the taxpayer over £800 million; aircraft development, where the estimate of Britain's share of Concorde is about £600 million; and computers, where government aid for research is expected to exceed £100 million. 'We have built up no export market in nuclear reactors . . . the research and development costs of the Concorde will not be recouped by sales . . . Our computer industry is not self-supporting.' He accuses the politicians of an almost neurotic reaction to the fear that other nations are hard on our heels and hence that we must spend more and more freely on high technology.

High technology, as defined by Jewkes, is quite simply high-risk technology; risky not, he argues, because of the technical uncertainties but because of *commercial* uncertainties. High technology implies 'projects to which companies, in close contact with realities, will not

[1] J. Jewkes, D. Sawers and R. Stillerman, *The Sources of Invention*, Macmillan, 1958.
[2] John Jewkes, *Government and High Technology*, Occasional Paper 37, Institute of Economic Affairs, p. 24.

give their support because the chances of profit seem too small, problematic or remote, but where the government, for one reason or another, feels that it knows better'. He concludes that the evidence provided by its handling of Concorde, or Rolls-Royce's RB.211 aero engine project, or nuclear reactor development, shows clearly that the government does not.

At first sight, Jewkes's case seems to be well supported by the record of support for invention by the government agency set up for this express purpose, the National Research Development Corporation. Take the fate of the bigger companies set up by NRDC during the 1960s to exploit an invention or technology. By the end of 1972 the British Hovercraft Corporation had faded away to become a wholly-owned subsidiary of Westland Aircraft. It cost Westland only £75,000 to buy the NRDC shareholding. There was a joint venture in 1961 by NRDC in partnership with three major industrial groups, British Petroleum, British Ropes and Guest Keen and Nettlefold, to develop Mr. Tom Bacon's ideas for fuel cells. By 1969 it was clear that there was more promise in a 'spin-off' idea from its research programme, for a new kind of primary cell. This 'spin-off' activity was subsequently sold off to GKN, with British Ropes and NRDC retaining minority holdings. The fuel cell meanwhile had turned out to be a much more complex and much less efficient machine than the straightforward 'battery with a fuel pipe' concepts of a decade before. Like hovercraft they can be purchased today but there is little demand for so complex a solution to energy storage problems. The industrial partners dropped out of the venture, and support for research was maintained at quite a low level by a wholly-owned NRDC subsidiary, Fuel Cells Limited.

A couple of NRDC ventures that made quite a stir when first announced are now moribund. Cammell Laird (Sea Bed Engineering), of which NRDC holds 49 per cent in partnership with the ship-building group, set out to develop a special tractor for service on the sea-bed. The tractor was never completed. Cynics say that the scheme was misbegotten—that at best it would have been a jolly fine way of stirring the mud and obliterating vision for sea-bed workers. The other venture now in cold storage was in cryogenics, the technology of extreme cold, where three industrial organisations, International Research and Development, Hymatic Engineering and Petrocarbon Developments joined NRDC in Cryosystems Ltd., a consortium for developing cryogenic tools and systems. In the mid-1960s the market potential seemed to stretch all the way from the operating table out into space. In fact, no substantial market ever materialised.

City crashes

It should be remembered, however, that in all of these ventures NRDC was supported by industrial partners of sound repute, each of whom lost money in the joint venture. In another joint venture that foundered the agency had the backing of one of the City's most highly respected merchant banks. In 1969 Kleinwort Benson brought together a group of financial institutions (they included the Church Commissioners and the Prudential) willing to put £5 million or so into an ambitious computer venture. Autonomics was essentially a computer software operation planned to provide other organisations with on-line access to powerful computers through specially tailored terminals and software. NRDC chipped in with £500,000. Autonomics crashed late in 1971. Kleinwort Benson itself called in the receiver when it discovered debts of around £6 million. I was present at an informal post-mortem when senior representatives of Kleinwort Benson and NRDC agreed it was partly their own fault for not keeping the two entrepreneurs behind Autonomics on a much tighter rein. 'We thought you were watching them,' said one shamefacedly. 'But we thought *you* were watching,' another replied.

The crash of Autonomics rattled the ornate glass panelling of almost every City finance house ever to show any interest in supporting science-based industries. The City had still not recovered from the crash of Rolls-Royce a few months before. Lazards, another renowned merchant bank, had loaned Rolls-Royce £2·5 million on the strength of its RB.211 aero-engine contract with Lockheed. So profound were these shocks to City bankers that they were avowing never again to touch technology. Mr. John Gillum, then a Kleinwort Benson director, was quoted as saying that the bank would say 'no' in future to any proposed combination of innovation and an unknown market. 'This is not our style and I am certain that others in the City will follow. The risks are very much greater than people believe.'[1]

So shaken, it seems, were the bankers that another, though smaller, crash late in 1972 raised scarcely a ripple. A company called Laser Associates, which in six years had grown to become Britain's biggest design and manufacturing group in the glamorous new technique of lasers, abruptly went broke, despite the fact that one of its two 'fairy godmothers' was a merchant bank of the standing of Hambros. Demand for its laser products never reached the level that would have covered the heavy development costs involved. It had debts of £600,000. What remained—designs, know-how, goodwill and so on —was sold to Ferranti for £100,000.

[1] *The Guardian*, 30 November 1971.

Early in the life of Laser Associates I had talked to Mr. Ray Wheeler, the director responsible for 'racing money' at Hambros 'Racing money' was the 10 per cent or so of the bank's venture capital investments that it allocated to new ideas. In those days (1968) it amounted to about £200,000 a year. 'We love racing,' said Wheeler, 'but we hit the market much more often with straight management backing. And we know a lot of our entrepreneurs will not listen to us in the long run.' But he emphasised that 'racing' was not something novel to the merchant bank, 'although now we are professional about it'. The criteria on which a scientist's proposition was assessed did not differ greatly from those used to judge anyone else's proposition. The bank had the technical *nous* to root out the complete non-starters—the ideas that flouted the laws of thermodynamics, for example. But by and large, even in 'racing', the bank was simply backing someone it judged above average in management ability to make a commercial success of his ideas in high technology.

In Laser Associates, Ray Wheeler thought he had found such a team; four men working in laser and microwave systems for a Joseph Lucas subsidiary, G. and E. Bradley, who felt they were getting too much interference and too little support—'a story we heard over and over again about big organisations', commented Wheeler. The four broke away and set up in a garage making lasers and laser systems. Hambros invested £50,000, taking 20 per cent of the equity. 'They convinced us,' said Wheeler, 'because they had a product and had already made some money, and because they added up to a team.' Inside two years of starting they were joined by another dissident group of laser experts from AEI who felt themselves threatened by the GEC takeover. By 1970 they had built up a team of sixty-five and a turnover in lasers and laser-based systems of £380,000.

In fact, the returns for successful 'racing' can be impressive— which provides the main attraction for entrepreneurs, banks and politicians alike. But inevitably the odds against success are fairly high. At the time it backed Laser Associates, Hambros estimated the odds no better than one chance in ten even for the schemes that had passed all their screens and duly received financial backing. For NRDC they must inevitably be higher for the state agency usually receives applications for finance from the private sector only after the entrepreneur has failed to find a commercial sponsor such as a manufacturing company or a merchant bank.

NRDC is treading a narrow path between the type of venture that merchant banks traditionally support, where the risk although higher than in straightforward commercial ventures is still fairly low, and the straight gamble with science where the odds against success are exceedingly high. It is trying to reconcile an intellectual attraction for the straight gamble with a statutory requirement to balance its books. *Figure 2* summarises twenty-five years of progress in which a total of 30,050 'brainwaves' submitted to the Corporation has been whittled down to 753 income-earning inventions. Yet Bill Makinson, its managing director, can still claim that he cannot, in eight years with NRDC, recall a single idea that 'got away' and made money for someone else.

At the merchant banking end of the risk spectrum NRDC tries to work whenever possible in partnership with the City. Even this does not guarantee success, as was plain from the failure of Autonomics. Neither, however, has it discouraged NRDC from another, similar but quite specific venture into specialised computer software—for stock-brokers. There are a dozen or more ventures in which NRDC at the time of writing (early 1974) is working with Technical Development Capital, the venture-capital arm of ICFC.

At the gambling end of the risk spectrum the Corporation is willing to chance comparatively small sums of public money on an immense diversity of schemes. An obvious proviso is that the idea should not flout basic laws of science (such as the second law of thermodynamics). Another, and often more crucial requirement is the traditional yardstick of any banker, that the inventor should be a person in whom the NRDC has reasonable confidence that he can make a success of the venture. As anyone who has close dealings with inventors knows well, it may not always be easy to discern commercial acumen. Rejection on this count alone tends to leave the corporation with a large number of outspoken critics scattered across the land.

The joint venture with industry accounts, however, for roughly half of the current projects and substantially more than half the finance committed. Half a dozen of these joint ventures lie in the £500,000–£2 million bracket, and a total of thirty-five have been allocated funds exceeding £100,000.

Summing up for me its experience over twenty-five years, upon his retirement as chief executive in 1974, Dr. Basil Bard said: 'One in three of everything we back fails completely—is a write-off. On one in three projects we get our investment back. With one project in three we are more successful than we had hoped.'

Where Jewkes is wrong

Where Professor Jewkes goes awry in his thesis is in equating high technology with high-risk venture, and in suggesting that only politicians and civil servants remote from the market are foolhardy enough to invest in such ventures. It was commercial not technical

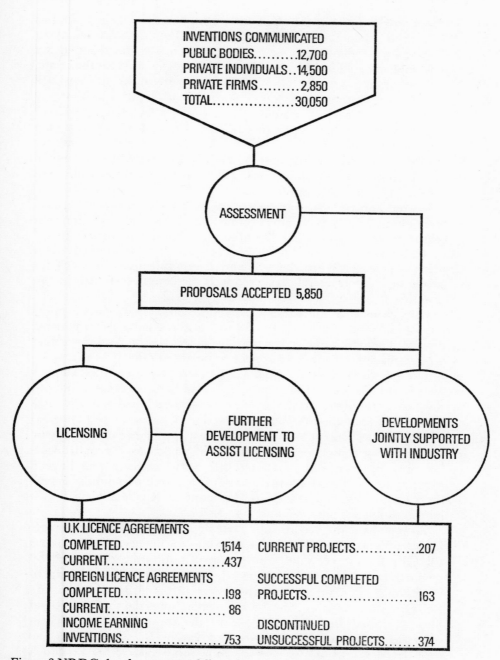

Figure 2 NRDC development and licensing activity 1949–1973.

misjudgment that cost 'Ma Bell', the giant American Telephone and Telegraph Corporation, at least $100 million (£40 million) in developing a video-telephone system. Technically, the product, the most sophisticated technical package yet to be invented for the home, was astonishingly successful. What the company failed to spot until it was deep into the jungle of 'negative cash flow' was that the market was simply not ready for it. Corfam, a technically brilliant imitation of leather, cost Dupont a cool $80m.–$100m. before the company acknowledged that the market had changed and most of the demand could be fulfilled either by leather itself or by much simpler and cheaper substitutes. What little remained could not justify a Dupont scale of operations.

Nearer home there was no technological risk whatsoever, and certainly no government intervention, in the 'racing' operation that cost Rowntree losses of £32·5 million in 1973 through speculations in the cocoa market. But I would argue that investment in a more sophisticated intelligence and communications network for cocoa speculators could have reduced the commercial risk in this situation.

Pharmaceutical companies accept odds that, at first glance, appear almost foolhardy, in their quest for major new chemicals for treating disease. The odds against any newly synthesised compound arriving on the pharmacist's shelves appear to be about one chance in 4,500 —and lengthening all the time. Total development costs for a major drug in Britain nowadays averages £3–4 million and some would put this figure still higher. If the drug has to be abandoned at a late stage in the research–development–production sequence—as happened when ICI in 1971 abandoned a new treatment for rheumatic disease because of a remote risk to women of jaundice—the entire outlay may be sacrificed. But success in drug research can have a big pay-off, with sales worth tens of millions of pounds a year for a major innovation, such as Hoffmann la Roche achieved with its tranquillisers.

To put the NRDC record into better perspective, its largest single source of income has been from royalties on licences to Glaxo and Eli Lilly for the cephalosporin group of antibiotics discovered by scientists at the University of Oxford. In awarding a Royal Medal to Professor E. P. Abraham, co-discoverer of the drug with the late Dr. G. C. F. Newton, Sir Alan Hodgkin, president of the Royal Society, called the research 'one of the most important British successes for many years' in drug research. By then (1973) the cephalosporin antibiotics were earning more than $200 million a year in world sales.

What, then, we are left with in the Jewkes case against high technology is an argument against government intervention in broadly three sectors where, quoting Lord Beeching, he accuses the politicians of 'an almost childlike desire to play with toys'. The three sectors are aviation, nuclear energy and computers. Personally, I have great sympathy with the remark of Lord Beeching, once made to the House of Commons Expenditure Committee. Would that his eminently sensible proposals of the mid-1960s for reshaping Britain's railways along modern lines had received the sort of sympathy MPs showed for the hovertrain project in 1973 when the government announced that it had been killed.

But Jewkes, in his lecture, almost completely ignored the basic reason for government support for aviation, nuclear energy and computers. In his Wincott Lecture he dismissed it in a mere 133 words under 'national interest'. It is, of course, the question of national security—security against military, economic or political assaults from outside and even within its own frontiers.

National security

Security, in this broad sense, is without question the primary role of government, of overriding importance. Without security the most ambitious programme for health, welfare or education have little meaning. One can—and must—question the individual decisions within the three high technologies. But that is a far cry from saying that government should leave the commercial world to decide whether and how the nation should pursue three high technologies that successive governments of very different political persuasion have all apparently agreed are fundamental to national security. Had the government intervened more determinedly in the ill-managed affairs of the nuclear industry in the 1960s, and at the same time allowed the private sector less freedom to grow so dependent on Middle East oil, Britain might have been much better cushioned against the events of late 1973, when the Arabs began to use oil as a political lever.

'People are not slow to turn the screw,' remarked Dr. Israel Dostrovsky, leading nuclear adviser to the Israeli Prime Minister, when I talked to him early in 1972 about Israeli ambitions for self-sufficiency in the same three high technologies. The USA, Britain and France had each attempted to bend Israel to its will by withholding some vital piece of advanced technology. As a result, Israel, which for some years had been tantalising these countries as well as its Arab neighbours with the possibility that it already had a nuclear weapon, in 1973 revealed that it did have some very advanced air-to-air missile technology entirely of its own creation.

The United States in the 1960s tried to bend General de Gaulle to its will by withholding a powerful IBM computer needed by the atomic energy commission (CEA) for the French nuclear weapons programme. It made France quite determined to remain in computers in competition with the US giants. The US had already tried to deprive Britain of nuclear weapons technology when, despite the wartime partnership of the two nations in the Manhattan Project, Congress in 1946 passed the McMahon Act which, to quote Professor Gowing, 'destroyed general Anglo-American collaboration in nuclear energy'.[1] The same year the post-war Labour government launched Britain's programme for an independent nuclear weapon.

Today the United States itself is one of many industrialised nations whose security is being threatened by the political ambitions of the oil-exporting nations of the Middle East. One reaction has been heavier US government spending in certain key areas of nuclear energy.

How to manage

The key question for government, I would suggest, is not whether but *how* it should be managing the three sectors of high technology. All three, but aerospace in particular, are fraught with danger for the taxpayer; danger that service chiefs abetted by politicians will go chasing after some sexy proposal that the scientist and engineers have hinted they believe is possible. In the 1960s in Britain it was TSR.2, the supersonic strike reconnaissance aeroplane. In the 1970s it may be a new submarine security system for the protection of a massive industrial investment on the bed of the North Sea. There may be an excellent case to be made for such a scheme—as there was for a Canberra replacement—but it must be much more tautly controlled. As later chapters will try to show, high technology can be controlled provided a few basic rules are followed.

All too easily, however, schemes in these three high technology sectors can stretch into 'prestige projects', where the reputation of a service arm or, worse, a government is at stake. All too easily such schemes tend to 'spin-off' others, ostensibly sound commercial projects claiming to put to good use the technology needed in the security sector. Britain's ideas for Concorde began modestly in this way, as we shall see in the following chapter. All too willingly industry, largely perhaps wholly dependent on government contracts in these high technologies, abdicates as a source of independent advice in the key decisions. If the project comes off it will earn credit and more

[1] Margaret Gowing, *Britain and Atomic Energy 1939–1945*, Macmillan, 1964.

contracts. If it fails it is the politicians who lose face. The pressures have been weighted too heavily in favour of continuing projects in these three industries—especially in the aerospace and nuclear industries—long after their usefulness has been called seriously into question.

B

CHAPTER 3

Aviation: a pampered industry

'Many learned that when men's lives are at stake it is a great mistake to quote the best performance your instruments will achieve.'
Prof. R. V. Jones, speaking at a Royal Society discussion on the effects of two world wars on science in Britain, 1974.

There's more money in the City than good propositions, is a cry often heard from merchant bankers. But let us be clear what the City regards as a 'good proposition'. One kind undoubtedly is the proposition where, if all else fails, the state will step in to pick up the bill. Add the glamour that heavier-than-air machines have held for the public for nearly seventy years now and you have a 'good proposition': the British aviation industry.

'Why on earth should this be?' I hear the reader protest. The industry has a laughable record of cost control. It offered us Concorde for £170 million and by 1973 the estimate exceeded £1,000 million. It offered us TSR.2 as a Canberra replacement— at twenty-five times the Canberra's cost. It offered us the RB.211 engine for £65·5 million and the research bill turned out to be nearly £200 million. We gave it the hovercraft to design and develop and, quoting a sardonic comment a senior defence scientist once made to me, 'we were offered a weapon at aircraft prices with a tenth of an aircraft's speed'.

None of this matters to the City, of course; or rather, all of it matters but simply to persuade the City that its money is pretty soundly invested. Governments may from time to time conclude that, as Mr. Roy Jenkins when Minister of Aviation so succinctly put it, 'the industry had reached the stage where it needed a few rude shocks'. Governments have even been rude enough to let aviation companies collapse—though only under extreme provocation. Most of the time successive governments have tolerated an industry which has consistently underestimated its research and development costs by a factor of more than three—and sometimes much more.

Let us look at the situation another way. In the first six months of office the Labour government of 1964 killed off three major aviation projects at various stages of development. The biggest was the TSR.2

strike reconnaissance aircraft, which had just made its first flight and by then was absorbing about £4 million a month in research and development costs. The others were the P.1154 supersonic 'jump-jet' and the HS.681 vertical take-off transport. Britain's airspace was thick with cries of 'murder'. (One highly emotional outburst published soon after by a politician with business connections with the industry was even entitled *The Murder of TSR-2.*) Now, one effect at least that these cancellations might have been expected to show was a sharp reduction in the research and development budget of the aircraft industry. The budget for 1964–5, the year before the cancellation, had been £139 million. But the budget for 1966–7, the year after the cancellations, had jumped to £153 million. The following year it was up again, £164 million.[1] The growth in research costs the industry had enjoyed before the slaughter was proceeding unchecked.

Need one wonder that the City loves an industry that can survive such traumas unscathed? If this is high technology, where is the risk?

No post-war British government has seriously challenged the assumption that the nation—for reasons of security—must have an aircraft industry of a certain minimum size. Aircraft and aerospace systems undoubtedly qualify as high technology. Spending on research and development probably exceeds 20 per cent. This makes research a major sub-section of the industry, under heavy and constant pressure from the defence sector to stretch engine, aircraft and avionics performance to ever greater heights. But beyond this, research and development costs are the price Britain is paying to keep a big aircraft industry alive.

Cockburn's Law

Sir Robert Cockburn, an outspoken physicist who was director of the Royal Aircraft Establishment at Farnborough until his retirement in 1970, points out one consequence of the situation. Cockburn's Law for the cost of an aircraft project in Britain is simple and brief:

$$\text{Project cost} = \frac{\text{Total aviation R \& D}}{n}$$

where n is the number of projects the government permits to proceed.[2] A corollary to this law is that development projects expand to absorb the total effort available.

[1] *R and D Performed within, or Financed by, Industry*, Central Statistical Office Study on Research and Development Expenditure, HMSO, 1973.
[2] The industry occasionally launches private ventures but rarely of any magnitude without the government's blessing—and its financial backing.

It is realistic, in my opinion, to regard the aircraft industry in Britain—or for that matter in any country outside the US and Russia —as essentially a research, development and design activity with some largish workshops where a few models may be turned out. It is certainly no less realistic than claiming that a nation which is selling Concorde and the RB.211 engine, its major civil aviation projects today, at a heavy loss has a commercially competitive aircraft industry. See it, however, as a research and design activity with a major mission in national security, and the aircraft industry begins to come into perspective. Accept how intense are the pressures for the defence sector to see how far aerodynamic and avionic concepts will stretch, and you begin to see the immense attraction for creative engineers and scientists. Add to this the glamour, the public appeal of the heavier-than-air machines, acknowledged by the number of correspondents in the news media who devote themselves wholly to the industry's activities, and you begin to see why it is always chasing —if never quite reaching—a pot of gold.

My favourite illustration of this argument is a brilliant British concept of vertical take-off for aircraft. Sir Sydney Camm's idea for an aircraft whose engine could provide either lift or thrust and a smooth transition from one to the other has an elegance and simplicity that puts it among the great inventions of aviation. It well illustrates, too, the first of Camm's four basic principles of design, one not always followed in aviation (or indeed in other technologies): 'See the need and set out to provide it.'[1]

Camm's ideas for using 'vectored thrust' were first publicly displayed at Farnborough in 1962 in a prototype vertical take-off fighter called the P.1127, already under development as a private venture by Hawker Siddeley since 1957. The P.1127 used a single engine for vertical take-off, hovering, forward propulsion and vertical descent. It did so by 'vectoring' or diverting the thrust from this engine by as much as ninety degrees. To this day no one has found a more graceful mode of vertical take-off. By 1963 the P.1127 was taking part in shipboard trials on the carrier *Ark Royal*, hovering in a 20-knot wind in Lyme Bay. Then, with excitement beginning to mount in the Services at home and overseas, the research effort began to shift. A new and more powerful aircraft had been conceived, the supersonic P.1154, equipped with a new and very advanced engine, the BS.100. Research and development interest focused on the new aircraft, despite the fact that its precursor remained a prototype without orders and with a huge number of problems to be solved before it could emerge as a credible fighting machine.

[1] R. L. Lickley, 'First Sir Sydney Camm Lecture', *Aeronautical Journal*, vol. 75, no . 724, April 1971.

Just how formidable those problems were the reader may gauge for himself from subsequent events. The P.1154 supersonic project was cancelled early in 1965, re-focusing the industry's interest on the P.1127 precursor. Control alone, for an aircraft wobbling insecurely atop its own thrust, presented problems for the computer that had never been tackled before. Slowly the concept progessed, through Kestrel (for which the RAF took first deliveries in 1965) to the Harrier warplane, which entered RAF squadron service in 1969. At the time of writing, the Royal Navy has still not committed itself to firm orders for an aircraft it first tried out at sea over ten years ago.

This question of lead time is a highly significant aspect of all high technology. Commerce has not yet adjusted to the idea that in this sector it can be ten years or more from the original idea until profits really begin to flow. A drug may take a decade from its discovery to profitability, and twelve years to reach peak earnings. But at least a drug-maker stands a fair chance of making good profits early in the commercial life-span of a new drug. For a new aero-engine or air-craft it can be as long as fifteen years because the manufacturer is earning peak profits from the venture only once he is selling a large volume of spare parts.

Rolls-Royce's troubles

Nothing highlights the eccentricities of this industry more starkly than the decline and fall of Rolls-Royce, as illuminated by the subsequent government investigation, which showed so clearly how huge sums of money can remain unproductive and at immense risk for very long periods.[1] Mostly, of course, it is the taxpayers' money: 70 per cent in the case of the RB.211 engine despite the fact that this was purely a civil aero-engine project, and such ventures normally rate no more than 50 per cent public support.

The RB.211 engine, technically an outstanding success, was nevertheless the project that caused the crash of Rolls-Royce, one of the most famous company names in the world. The crash, early in 1971, had consequences that were far-reaching. Its paramount importance as a defence contractor obliged a government ideologically opposed to nationalisation to take the company into state-ownership. It sorely damaged the credibility of scientists and engineers with the City. It destroyed, temporarily at least, the prospects for a new engineering material capable of advancing a vast number of traditional British engineering products whose markets are threatened increasingly by competition overseas.

[1] *Rolls-Royce Limited*, Report of the Department of Trade and Industry, HMSO, 1973.

The first two consequences have already been debated exhaustively by the Press. Let us look at the project from the point of view of the third consequence, its effect on another British invention, carbon fibre.

Early in the 1960s Rolls-Royce, one of the world's three great aero-engine companies and the leading innovator in this sector, recognised the need for a big new engine for a new generation of wide-bodied aircraft the airlines were contemplating, and they envisaged engines of up to 50,000lb. thrust, compared with the 22,000lb. of its Conway engine. In 1963 Mr. A. A. Lombard, Rolls-Royce's director of engineering, was making his case to the Board for work to begin on a big engine. Two years later he began building a 'demonstrator' engine called the RB.178, designed to give 28,500lb. thrust.

But Lombard, an outstanding engineer by any standard, became convinced that he could design an engine of far greater thrust by having three instead of the customary two shafts. His third shaft, although inevitably a complication for his designers, would also afford a new dimension of economy and control. If successful, the three-shaft concept would leapfrog the big high-bypass engines already well under development in the US.

Meanwhile, the company completed its two-shaft RB.178 demonstrator engine and achieved 93 per cent of its design thrust. But the big machine revealed some serious mechanical faults. Once the three-shaft RB.211 project was under way its precursor programme was dropped—as an economy measure. It proved—long afterwards—a false economy, as the inquiry learned after the crash. The £1·5 million RB.178 programme could, had it continued, have solved some of the RB.211's problems up to two years earlier. Sir David Huddie, managing director of Rolls-Royce's aero-engine division at the time, told the inquiry very frankly that it was 'one of our great mistakes'.

Rolls-Royce in the 1960s was dominated by first-class engineers like Huddie and his chairman Sir Denning Pearson—the two men at whose door the inquiry laid much of the blame for the crash. But the man who shoulders a huge burden in any organisation operating at the frontiers of engineering development is the chief engineer. He walks the knife-edge between the design that is impossible to achieve on the time-scale and to the price demanded, and one that falls short of the possible—and perhaps of the competition.

Lord Hinton, who walked this knife-edge for a decade after the war while building Britain's atomic factories, calls creativity in a designer the 'divine discontent that makes him feel that there must be some better way of doing things than the way that has been used in the past and that it is worthwhile taking calculated risks to find the better way'. Hinton believes young design engineers should be taught poker as part of their training in taking decisions. In poker, as in creative engineering design, there are things you know for certain, things you think you know, and things you don't know—and know you can't know. Wait until you know everything for certain and your decision will achieve very little. 'On the other hand, you have to be sure that when you go beyond the limits of your knowledge the risk that you take is justified and you have to be sure the stake is one you can afford.'[1]

Lombard's decision

The truly creative hand at Rolls-Royce at this time was that of Adrian Lombard, director of engineering from 1958. Here was the man with the flair for the degree of technical risk the company could run; who could spot the point when the risk grew too great. Under his guidance the company had been developing an entirely novel technology for making jet engines from plastics. Reinforced with strong fibres and cleverly fashioned so as to maximise their assets and minimise drawbacks, plastics were proving the equal of metals—and potentially very much lighter and cheaper to fashion. Lombard's goal at first was a jet engine for an entirely new purpose: one that would provide an aircraft with vertical lift but would be so much dead weight once the aircraft was on its way, propelled by a more conventional power plant. Lombard was striving for the simplest and lightest lift engine he could design. He went so far as an engine with a thrust-to-weight ratio of 16 to 1—astonishingly high—by making 40 per cent of it from reinforced plastics.

Lombard drew heavily on this 'composite materials' technology when he came to design the RB.211. What is more, he endorsed another major leap forward, by using as reinforcement for plastic engine components not the fibres of glass used in the lift engines but fibres of carbon, stronger and five or six times as stiff. Scientists at Rolls-Royce's own advanced research laboratory near Derby had found the way of making such fibres. Confidence was further reinforced by parallel work—subsequently acknowledged as still more advanced and antedating the Rolls-Royce effort—at the Royal Aircraft Establishment, Farnborough.

Lombard quickly became convinced that, radical though the departure from accepted engineering practice was the very idea of 'plastic engines', carbon-reinforced plastics could be used extensively in the big new engine. He talked of making the front bearing housing

[1] Lord Hinton, *Engineers and Engineering*, Oxford University Press, 1970, pp. 36–40.

assembly, the high-pressure compressor casing, about half the high-pressure rotor and stator blades and the bypass duct—all major engine components—from reinforced plastic. Above all he proposed to use plastics in the big fan.

The fan of a big high-bypass engine is a truly formidable engineering challenge. From this one component the RB.211 was to obtain 70 per cent of its thrust. In the fan the designer perceived what Stephen Bragg, as chief scientist of Rolls-Royce, later came to call the 'ecological niche' for carbon-fibre reinforced plastics. Its huge blades, nearly three feet in length and a foot across at the tip, would spin at a top speed calculated to tax the endurance of the strongest metals. They had to be light because of their size, yet had to resist dislocation and deformation under immense centrifugal or stretching forces. Lombard narrowed the choice of material for these blades to two lightweight but strong substances: titanium and Hyfil, Rolls-Royce's carbon-reinforced plastic. On paper Hyfil offered an impressive advantage; blades only one-third of the weight, which in turn improved specific fuel consumption by 1 per cent. Lombard chose Hyfil, a courageous decision, unpopular with the metallurgists at Rolls-Royce who had served the company so well in the past.

That decision, typical of high-technology situations, committed the company to a course of action on the grounds that when the time came to show its hand commercially, it would have all the right answers. It is a flair for taking this sort of risk—and winning—that distinguishes the great from the good engineer. Lombard's decision launched an immense technical effort to transfer a brand-new material from the laboratory into an airliner on a time-scale never attempted before. But in July 1967, when only fifty-two, Adrian Lombard died suddenly before even the big Lockheed order was landed. His death left a yawning gap in the top management of Rolls-Royce. 'A powerful leader and a first-rate designer, head and shoulders above his subordinates', recorded the subsequent inquiry. Many witnesses averred that the RB.211's manifold problems would have been less troublesome had he lived.

How Hyfil failed

Let us continue to follow one of those problems—one of the biggest, though perhaps I should emphasise by no means the only technical problem raised by the revolutionary RB.211 design. (Rolls-Royce afterwards isolated twelve aspects in which its design involved a significant technical advance.) The significance of the Hyfil decision, however, was that in engineering terms it was, as an unproven material in an extremely demanding situation, the greatest single risk in the entire project—and recognised as such right from the start.

Hyfil subsequently succumbed to birds; a tragedy that left a remarkable new material tainted and deprived engineers of an outstanding British invention (*see chapter 9*). But so much was at stake with the RB.211 programme that subsequent reaction against carbon-fibre seems almost inevitable. Let there be no idea, however, that the bird problem took Rolls-Royce by surprise. By the summer of 1968, when the RB.211 programme for Lockheed was under way, the 'bird hazard', to quote one engineer I talked to then, had already begun to 'loom like a mountain'. The problem is simply that the huge fan of the high-bypass design of engine acts as an immensely powerful vacuum cleaner, sucking in such things as rain or hailstones, grit from the runway—and birds. These batter the big fan blades with immense force. Rolls-Royce's own specification for the RB.211 called for a resistance to bombardment by 4lb. birds—such as a biggish wild goose—striking the leading edge of the fan blade. At take-off, when the engine is developing maximum thrust, such a blow is roughly equivalent to a Mini striking the blade at 30m.p.h.

The 'bird hazard' thus exposes the fan blade to stresses of a totally different nature from those that led Lombard to select Hyfil. The carbon fibres in Hyfil provide immense strength and stiffness along its length to resist the centrifugal forces trying to stretch the blades, even tear them from their roots. But a blow from a bird imposes stresses in a quite different direction—twisting forces at the root, for example—in which the material has little capacity to absorb the stress. So large loomed the problem by July 1968 that the Board was urged by its own engineers to launch a back-up development programme for a hollow blade of titanium, the only alternative to Hyfil that would not demand a major re-design of the engine. A year later, however, progress with the Hyfil blade was about the one bright spot in the development programme. Ernest Eltis, who had replaced Lombard as chief engineer, was telling his Board on 1 September 1969 of his concern for 'the slow progress in achieving a satisfactory engine standard'. But the Hyfil fan blade had made such good progress that he believed the titanium blade back-up programme could be dropped. Lockheed, moreover, had endorsed this decision.

Alas, it was a decision reached under the pressures of trying to arrest runaway research and development costs (*see table 2*). Tom Metcalfe, RB.211 programme controller—a Cassandra compared with the confidence exuded by some of his senior colleagues that all would turn out for the best in the end—was warning his managing director David Huddie later that year that there were serious problems lurking 'just under the surface' that would come to light only when they began to run engines hard for fairly long spells. And the Hyfil blade could prove to be one of those problems.

Table 2   RB.211–22 engine launch cost estimates

	Estimated launch cost to 2 years in service	Total launch cost including on-going development
1968 (Sept.)	£74·9m	£89·3m
1969 (June)	£84·1m	£99·6m
1970 (Jan.)	£91·5m	£107·8m
1970 (March)	£119·1m	£134·7m
1970 (April)	£119·1m	£151·8m
1970 (July)	£136·7m	£169·2m
1970 (Sept.)	£137·5m	£170·3m
1971 (18 Jan.)	£160·3m	£202·7m
1971 (25 Jan.)	£154·2m	£195·2m

In January 1970—less than six months after the back-up blade programme had been stopped—work on a titanium fan blade was re-started. Hyfil's twin problems at that stage were seen as weakness of the blade root, where the blade joins the disc or hub, and the 'bird hazard'. There was simply no way of keeping birds out of the engine without reducing its efficiency catastrophically.

Within two months disaster struck Hyfil. On a test run outdoors the big fan shed at least one of its blades, the blade root itself failing. Debris striking adjacent blades caused them to fail too, in a 'domino effect' of the kind engineers dread. Loss of blades unbalanced the stresses on the engine causing the fan shaft to break. A length of shaft shot out like a shell for some sixty yards. As the inquiry records, confidence in the composite blade was severely shaken—so much so that Hyfil was promptly abandoned. Whatever the cost in performance and price, the blades of the first RB.211 engines for Lockheed had to be of titanium.

Just how profound this change of plan was for the project is readily shown. On the time scale allowed there could be no possibility of simply substituting a hollow metal component for the wretched Hyfil blades. The hollow metal blade itself still called for a long and costly development programme. The alternative had to be a solid, forged blade of titanium, more costly and—much more important—much heavier than the Hyfil blade. A heavier blade demanded a stronger containment ring round the fan, the 'armour plate' that prevents any debris from fan damage from penetrating the aircraft itself. Stainless steel would be needed instead of an aluminium ring, increasing still further the weight problem with an engine already overweight before Hyfil had failed.[1]

The cost of these changes, it was estimated that spring, would be a cool £13 million. The extra unit production cost for an engine scheduled to go into production that summer would be £12,000: up from £205,380 to £217,338. (The original estimate, made soon after Rolls-Royce landed the Lockheed contract, had been £153,655.) Launch costs for the engine had risen by now to an estimated £151·8 million.

This wasn't the end of the story, of course. Here was a project with an apparently insatiable thirst for funds. By the following January, just before the crash, the estimated production cost of the engine had increased to £282,000—and £44,000 was being attributed to modifications of the fan and its casing. What was worse, Rolls-Royce was broke. 'There can be no doubt', found the government inquiry in 1973, 'that the effective cause of the crash was the drain on the company's finances brought about by the RB.211 project.' Asked to put in a single sentence what went awry, the RB.211 programme director at the time of the crash said he could not improve on the statement: 'We failed to appreciate it was going to cost us so much.'

Optimism factor

Yet the record of aviation development is one in which development costs normally exceed original estimates by a formidable factor; an 'optimism factor' averaging more than three in Britain and sometimes reaching five or higher. It is true that Rolls-Royce could point to the remarkably successful way it had controlled development costs for the Spey engine in the early 1960s (*see also chapter 6*); but important though this development was, it simply was not a venture into the unknown like the RB.211, where the engineers expected to make and break a great many engines before they would get the configuration right.

The crash of Rolls-Royce differed from the fate of many other innovative organisations all over the world, that place so much faith in a single project, in only one important respect: the size of the industrial infrastructure this project was supporting. Many subcontractors in turn were wholly committed to Rolls-Royce. The £47 million the government granted as launching aid for this purely civil project was an exceptionally high proportion (70 per cent) of estimated development costs. But the grant left no loop-hole for

[1] Four years later, in the autumn of 1974, Rolls-Royce (1971) were planning crucial new tests on a redesigned fan using carbon fibre blades.

Rolls-Royce should those costs rise. The company was committed to pick up all of the extra cost. So we have a situation where a company commits itself not merely to a project with a very high technical risk but to one on which the company's whole future is founded. Only in aviation would you meet this situation in a large and well-established trading organisation: in the 1960s with English Electric Aviation and the TSR–2 warplane, for example, and now with British Aircraft Corporation and Concorde.

The inference surely is plain. Rolls-Royce's top management always felt confident that, if all else failed, the government would step in—as it had so often before in this industry—and shoulder the burden in the interests of national security. Step in it did, but at a price the Rolls-Royce Board never dreamed it would be asked to pay.

The point I must emphasise in this chapter is simply that the aviation industry in Britain, in attempting to make a commercial case for its existence, should fool no one nowadays. The record is too long and too damning. Of the six civil aircraft projects the industry launched between the end of the Second World War and 1960—all with government backing—the taxpayer got back more than he donated from one project only, the Viscount airliner. The Princess flying boat and the Rotodyne VTOL airliner were both abandoned by the government itself; other government work saved their makers from bankruptcy. Between them, the Britannia and Comet airliners, which did enter service, cost the taxpayer about £8 million. The sixth project was the Twin Pioneer, which succeeded in breaking even.

The sums involved were modest enough when compared with those of today. But during the 1960s aircraft and their engines rose very rapidly in sophistication and cost. Not only were they growing in size and speed, but greater 'availability'—such as all-weather flying —was being demanded by the airlines. Meanwhile the growing congestion in the air was greatly increasing the risks, which had to be countered with much more instrumentation.

Concorde

Which brings us to Concorde, the most advanced civil aviation project to come to fruition in the Western World, and like the RB.211 engine an astonishing technical achievement. Here was a project which, even when first announced late in 1962, was recognised as needing more cash than all its civil predecessors put together. The first estimate of the cost of developing Concorde as an Anglo-French project was £160–£170 million. (This compares with an estimated £60 million spent altogether on research and development of the Comet, the world's first turbo-jet airliner.) A decade later Concorde's estimated development costs had reached £1,065 million—a sixfold increase—and the aircraft was still two years from flight certification. Already over £700 million had been spent. How this cost has risen is indicated in *table 3*. Why it has risen—except for some £330 million attributed to inflation and devaluation—is still regarded as a state secret by the two nations. Apart, however, from the cost of meeting environmental objections, one might reasonably guess that quite a few problems which were never anticipated, and for which no contingencies were ever made in the original estimates, emerged as the project progressed.

How could a project which—as conceived by the British at least—was to exploit two major developments already existing in Britain run so far out of control? The original British concept for a supersonic transport was to make use of an engine, the Olympus, already under development for the TSR–2 warplane, and some excellent metallurgy in aluminium at Farnborough. The metallurgy showed that a supersonic airframe could be made of this metal instead of titanium, the US choice but a costly and troublesome metal of which Europe had little experience.

This question of control tormented the House of Commons Committee of Public Accounts, which in July 1973 reported that, in the absence of any clear indications of either sales prospects or the production costs if sales were low, the Concorde project was 'as speculative as it ever was'. Its report warned that unless there were more orders—the position then was firm orders for sixteen aircraft—the taxpayer would not only fail to see any return on his £1,065 million flutter but would have to meet losses 'which could be large' on each aircraft produced.

The Committee of Public Accounts made no attempt to disguise its annoyance and frustration at the secrecy with which the British government surrounded the breakdown of costs of the project. But it managed to separate the estimated increase due to inflation (£307 million); leaving nearly £600 million as the cost of development work the project had failed to anticipate (or failed to disclose) at the outset. The engine alone had absorbed £260 million in work by Rolls-Royce and SNECMA—a figure hard to reconcile with the original idea of using the TSR.2 engine.

Roger Williams, in a recent study of the politics of collaboration in high technology, observes that 'the weakness at the outset was that the Anglo-French agreement had to be entered into before the time at which, had the project been wholly British, the Ministry responsible would have been prepared to award a development contract'.[1] For that reason the initial estimate was little more than

[1] Roger Williams, *European Technology*, Croom Helm, 1973, p. 115.

Table 3 Anglo-French Concorde development cost estimates
(official figures)

	£ million	
1962 (Nov.)	150–170	(a)
1964 (July)	275	(b)
1966 (June)	450	(c)
1969 (May)	730	(d)
1970 (Jan.)	730	
1970 (Oct.)	825	
1971 (May)	885	
1972 (May)	970	
1973 (June)	1,065	(e)

(a) Regarded as pessimistic by French, probably optimistic by British.
(b) Included £40m. for changed requirements.
(c) Included £80m. for work after certificate of air-worthiness has been granted.
(d) Included £150m. for 'additional tasks'; £40m. for devaluation effects.
(e) Breaks down into the following work sectors:

Airframe: £640 million

Design	£130m
Testing (systems and structures)	£ 90m
Equipment development	£ 50m
Tooling	£100m
Aircraft manufacture	£ 90m
Flight tests	£ 80m
Miscellaneous other items	£100m
Total	£640m

Engine: £425 million

Bench development	£180m
Flight development	£ 80m
Exhaust system:	
1. bench development	£100m
2. flight development	£ 35m
Production tooling	£ 30m
Total	£425m

an inspired guess, for a project which turned out to be second in complexity only to the American space programme. (The cost of landing man on the moon, by the way, fell within the estimate made at the outset, $20,000–24,000 million.) In fact, the cost of developing Concorde can be explained in only one way. It is the price that Britain and France have been willing to pay to keep two of the world's great aviation companies, British Aircraft Corporation and Aerospatiale, in existence. As we shall see in chapter 6, it is really the price we must pay for fully employing people—at every level—more skilled at adding value to metal than those of any other industry.

CHAPTER 4

Nuclear engineering: a neglected industry

'The battle of nuclear power versus coal began as far as I was concerned in October 1960, the month that I took up my post as Chairman Designate of the Coal Board.'

Lord Robens, in his autobiography *Ten Year Stint*, 1972

Early in 1971 the name Peter Vinter began to appear in the British Press. Vinter, a diminutive and disarmingly affable fellow with a first in mathematics from Cambridge, had been a third secretary at the Treasury until 1969, when he was given responsibility for energy policy at the (then) Department of Trade and Industry.[1] He took charge of a committee—later known as the Vinter Committee—that had been asked by the government to decide which nuclear reactor the British electricity generating boards should be buying. The choice lay between more of the same British designs, a more advanced British reactor or a reactor licensed from overseas. The nuclear industry waited . . . and waited. *The Times* even published a leader under the headline 'Waiting for Vinter' which caused much amusement in the corridors of power when pinned to a notice board outside the office of Vinter's boss, above a picture of a scantily-clad lady lying in a cornfield.

But there was no hurry, inquirers were told, for the electricity generating boards with fourteen nuclear stations in operation or under construction were in no hurry to order more. Their own growth of electricity sales had been curtailed by the country's poor economic performance and by the resurgence of the gas industry during the 1960s. To get the decision right, everyone said sagely, was much more important than taking it quickly.

In fact, by the beginning of 1972 Vinter's committee had reached some very important conclusions. One was that no more advanced gas-cooled reactors (AGRs) should be ordered until the generating boards had one operating, so manifold were the problems that had been encountered in building the AGR stations.

[1] Formerly the Ministry of Technology (Mintech).

But a still more profound conclusion was to emerge from its deliberations. The reason why they were finding it so hard to choose between five or six reactors on the basis of past experience in Britain, was that the nuclear industry itself was in no shape to make a success of building *any* reactor. It was under-financed, ill-managed and lacked the motivation to make a success of a very complex engineering task. Get the industry right, it was concluded, and a clear decision on the choice of reactor would follow. Instead of an industry that was no more than a sub-contractor to the generating boards, the industry must be strengthened to produce an organisation capable of talking on equal terms with its customers. From an equitable 'customer–contractor relationship' would emerge in time the product that suited both parties best, on terms that would offer the contractor much more incentive to make a success of his task.

What went wrong?

Where had Britain, the nation which pioneered the exploitation of nuclear energy in the 1950s, gone so sadly awry in its efforts to capitalise on a very large research investment? Why was it that the nation that made such a resounding success of the Calder Hall station, bringing its first reactor on power in less than three years, has never built a commercial nuclear power station on time and to the contracted performance and price?

Since 1945, when the Labour government decided that Britain must develop its own nuclear weapons, the nation has spent about £1,200 million on nuclear research and development, initially through the Ministry of Supply but from 1955 through the UK Atomic Energy Authority. For this sum Britain has acquired:

1. Nuclear weapons of a design sufficiently advanced for the government to barter details with the US, in exchange for the nuclear explosive uranium-235.
2. One of the four nuclear submarine fleets of the world.
3. A profitable fuel company with earnings exceeding £60 million in 1973–4, and a reputation for its products unmatched anywhere in the world.
4. First-generation nuclear power (magnox) stations which, since 1971, have been generating electricity more cheaply than the best fossil-fuel plants operating in Britain.

What this expenditure has failed to achieve, however, is:

1. To raise any power from its second-generation (AGR) stations, hotter and more highly rated than their predecessors.[1]

[1] The first power from the AGRs is expected from Hinkley B in 1975.

2. To produce a reactor sufficiently attractive in capital cost to sell outside Britain.
3. To produce any commercial reactor on time and to the estimated price.

Why the disparity in performance between two sets of problems when the success stories were, if anything, more difficult technically than the failures? Personally, I don't think the answer is very different from that which emerged in the previous chapter, on the aircraft industry. Once more the best available talent has been captivated by essentially research and development problems. In fuel manufacturing, as well as in reactor technology, the processes are sufficiently novel and science-based to hold the attention of highly-qualified technical people. The same teams made a great success of building a series of prototype reactors and production units, including the Calder Hall and Chapelcross nuclear power plants, progenitors of the first British commercial stations. Comparatively few of these people, however, were willing to tackle the problems of engineering a series of large commercial nuclear stations—there were always too many fresh ideas to be explored for advancing reactor technology.

To understand how this great division between research and industry arose we need to look back nearly twenty years to the mid-1950s. Calder Hall, the world's first nuclear power station, designed to produce both plutonium-239 explosive and electricity, was nearing completion—although construction began only in 1953. The government of the day, delighted with the rapid progress of the new technology, produced a White Paper in 1955 which laid the foundations of Britain's—indeed the world's—first nuclear power programme.[1]

The 'men of Calder'—such men as John Cockcroft, Christopher Hinton and Bill Owen—who had carried out the research, design and project management for a whole series of novel nuclear factories, culminating in Calder Hall, were to become part of an independent agency called the UK Atomic Energy Authority, set up in 1955 with 20,000 employees. No research programme in energy or any other sector in Britain had ever commanded such resources before.

Calder Hall was a military plant with a by-product of electricity (used, in fact, at the nearby Windscale Works of the UK AEA). But so impressed was the government with its completion in little more than three years, and the promise it held as an alternative to coal (on which Britain was then almost wholly dependent for central electricity supplies), that it 'cooked the books' a little to justify a decision. In 1955 the best estimate of the cost of electricity from more stations

[1] *A Programme of Nuclear Power*, Cmnd. 9389, 1955.

of the Calder Hall type was one old penny a unit (kWh). This was much higher than the cost of electricity from coal or imported oil, because of the high cost of building reactors. But, like Calder, the commercial nuclear stations would have a by-product of plutonium, which was potentially valuable as a fuel for a future generation of reactors. In the White Paper of 1955, laying down Britain's first nuclear programme, it was simply assumed that the value of this plutonium by-product was 0·4 penny a unit. By happy chance this brought the net cost of nuclear electricity down to 0·6 penny a unit— the same cost as coal and oil.

This was not the only unsupported assumption the White Paper made. Another arose because its cost-estimates for commercial nuclear stations had been based on design studies, not on firm tenders. But the commercial stations would have to be built not by a small band of enthusiasts working under military pressures—and in great secrecy—but to normal commercial contracts by industry. The difference turned out to be profound.

Nevertheless the government embarked in 1955 on a modest programme of nuclear construction. The plan was to build a dozen small stations—that is, small by present-day standards—similar in output to Calder, over the next ten years. They were to generate 1,500–2,000mw of electricity—equivalent to five million tons of coal a year. Had the government been content to leave it at this, all might have been well, for the programme and the reactors themselves were of a size that gave Britain's heavy engineering industry a fair chance of feeling its way to success with a novel and much more difficult technology. Unfortunately, in the panic following the Suez crisis of 1956, when it feared for the security of oil supplies, it expanded the programme overnight to three times its previous size: 5,000–6,000mw by 1965.

The fact that the expansion delighted not only the newly created UK AEA but the heavy electrical and engineering industries, which scrambled to invest in the fledgling technology, does not exonerate the government from a serious misjudgment. The government failed to recognise just how difficult a task it was asking industry to undertake, and how ill-prepared industry was in terms of finance and skilled resources to shoulder the task. What is more, it had minimised industry's chances of acquiring skilled resources by creating on very alluring terms the UK AEA itself. In the US, where precisely the same difficulties were encountered in harnessing nuclear physics for power generation, the companies primarily involved were vastly bigger and stronger financially, but were also assisted enormously with research, development and design contracts, and a large amount of military business for US Navy reactors.

The sudden expansion of Britain's nuclear programme had another serious consequence in that it infuriated the coal industry, which saw nuclear power simply in terms of the loss of 10,000 jobs in the pits for each 2,000mw of nuclear reactors. The ensuing battle (see the quotation from Lord Robens at the start of this chapter) hurt nuclear power without ameliorating the miners' position. There was no man of Robens's stature and political skill to speak up for nuclear power. In 1960 the government, responding to increasing coal and oil supplies, slackened the pace of nuclear progress by 'stretching' the programme to 5,000mw by 1968.[1]

The consortium system

Hinton, managing director of the industrial group of the UK AEA and the man responsible for the design and construction of all of Britain's nuclear 'factories' until 1957, had recognised clearly enough what problems industry would meet with the nuclear power programme. Largely on his advice the government was encouraging industry to group itself into consortia. These were groups of four or five companies that would bring together the diverse engineering skills a nuclear station demanded, so overcoming the handicaps of the small size and resources of Britain's electrical companies at that time. Each of the initial consortia was headed by one of Britain's leading electrical companies.

But the consortia system was a theoretical solution to a real commercial problem. While each nuclear consortium would be in receipt of orders worth many millions of pounds, in practice they proved, as one executive put it to me much later, 'highly transparent to cash'. Money simply flowed through the consortium to its chief sub-contractors, who, of course, were its shareholders. For the same reason the consortium structure cannot bring to bear on its subcontractors normal commercial pressures to keep down the price or to meet delivery dates.

The question is worth asking whether the atom's complexities could have been accommodated by British industry in some other way, say by the chemical or aircraft industries. ICI, which dominated the chemical industry, had played a big and crucial role in the early stages, with its wartime work on uranium refining and enrichment, novel engineering materials and other problems. But already threatened with nationalisation by the post-war Labour government, the company reasoned that a major commitment to nuclear energy would merely increase the risk. It made a deliberate decision to stay clear.

[1] *The Nuclear Power Programme*, Cmnd. 1083, 1960.

Another industry with great resources, owing to the huge wartime expansion, and also well accustomed to working both with scientists and with government, was aviation. Technically, I have no doubt, this industry would have handled the atom with far greater aplomb than the clumsily contrived consortia, where key components— notably the boilermakers—were far too primitive in their technical skills for the new technology. In materials technology alone, the nuclear industry has needed to be even more adventurous than aviation, taming and using in very stressful situations such substances as uranium, graphite and new ceramics for which there was no previous engineering experience. Cost might have been another matter. As we shall see in chapter 6, aviation projects have a disturbing tendency to over-run their initial cost estimates by a very big factor. At least the cost of Britain's first nuclear power programme—which turned out to be just eight stations, all different—kept within 25 per cent of the price quoted.

Decline and fall of the consortia

It took a second British nuclear power programme to fully reveal the weaknesses of the consortia system and the inefficiency of a sharp division between R & D and design and construction. But by the end of 1973 Arthur Hawkins, the chairman of the Central Electricity Generating Board, was telling a parliamentary select committee that the four advanced gas-cooled reactor (AGR) stations the CEGB had ordered from three consortia at an estimated cost of £500 million were going to cost at least £900 million. 'A catastrophe that must not be repeated' he asserted when giving reasons why his Board wished to abandon any plans for building further AGR stations, or indeed any other British design of reactor, and switch instead to importing US reactor technology. The US technology would be licensed through the newly created National Nuclear Corporation, a single design and construction organisation dominated by Sir Arnold Weinstock, managing director of GEC, which was to absorb and replace the hapless consortia.

Let us leave for the moment the question of whether such a savage indictment of Britain's nuclear progress was fair, and try to trace briefly how the industry had contrived a cost over-run of aviation industry proportions. We must start with the government's decision in March 1957 to expand Britain's first nuclear power programme.[1] It was taken, remember, not because the estimated price of nuclear electricity had fallen, but in response to fears for oil and coal supplies. In effect it committed the CEGB to 5,000–6,000MW of uneconomic

[1] *Capital Investment in the Coal, Gas and Electricity Industries,* Cmnd. 132, 1957.

nuclear power. Hinton, who in 1957 left the UK Atomic Energy Authority and became chairman of the CEGB, took an engineer's decision to try to minimise the economic penalty on the Board's finances. He tried to make each successive station less uneconomic— by increasing its size and by incorporating the latest results of research and development. Therefore, instead of the dozen Calder-size reactors[1] envisaged in the 1955 programme, the generating boards ordered reactors of up to 600MW. Each station ordered was a different design—the last two radically different in as much as they used a pre-stressed concrete pressure vessel instead of the steel vessels of the earlier stations, allowing reactor size to be increased appreciably. Each station used a different design of fuel. Each station, in short, was a prototype.

But the government's decision in 1957 had another still more far-reaching consequence. It put immense pressure on the generating boards to seek a more economic type of nuclear reactor. Once again the UK AEA was only too eager to oblige. It had been working on a hotter, more highly rated version of the first-generation gas-cooled reactors, called the advanced gas-cooled reactor (AGR). The AGR used enriched instead of natural uranium fuel to obtain its greater thermal rating and hence—theoretically—its lower capital cost per kilowatt. The UK AEA had another reason for pressing the AGR as an early replacement for the magnox system, for it was keen to break into the business of uranium enrichment, on the back of a highly successful post-war military enrichment programme.

The consortia, however, were decidedly less sanguine about the AGR. Some of their shareholders—notably the civil engineers—had done well out of the magnox programme with its massive investment in concrete, but the consortia themselves were in pretty poor shape. One, Atomic Power Construction, had already received a mortal blow in 1963[2] when the CEGB decided to award the contract for the second 600MW reactor at Wylfa, last of the magnox contracts, to the same consortium that was building the first Wylfa reactor. It was about the closest the nuclear industry came in the course of this programme to 'replication', the idea that all parties should agree quickly on a standardised design of reactor and order this design in sufficient numbers to give industry a chance to reap benefits from economies of larger-scale manufacture. But this was no consolation for APC, which found itself without a new contract and, very soon after, without its chief shareholder, GEC.

From the standpoint of the industry constructing nuclear stations

[1] Calder Hall's reactors are about 50MW; the first commercial reactors were 100–150MW.

[2] The consortium was then called United Power Constructors.

the AGR was not particularly attractive. As a gas-cooled system like its precursor, magnox, it was bound to be high in capital cost, simply because it needs a much bigger volume of gas than of liquid to extract a given amount of heat from a nuclear reaction. The higher the capital cost, the harder it would be to sell overseas in competition with the US industry and its very compact water-cooled reactor designs. If it failed to sell overseas it would remain beholden to the domestic generating boards, which had shown scant sympathy with industry's problems and little desire to let it make reasonable profits. Neither did the industry feel any great loyalty towards the UK AEA and its aspirations. The UK AEA had made no great effort to transfer technology and experience to the private sector. Moreover, it had no intention of parting with the fuel side of the business. Nuclear fuel, it foresaw, could eventually become a very lucrative business, analogous to the relationship King Gillette recognised back in 1895 between razor blades and the safety razor. Fuel services can be worth at least as much as the reactor contract over the lifespan of the reactor.

What the consortia wanted to do was to license US designs of water-cooled reactors. Although there was no commercial operating experience to compare with Britain's magnox reactors, all the evidence was that these designs could be constructed more cheaply than gas-cooled reactors. This would be a strong selling point to privately owned electrical utilities around the world, even if the overall cost of generation worked out much the same as for the AGR. What is more, the consortia would have the backing of the licensor, which meant companies of the size and reputation of US General Electric and Westinghouse Electric.

What the consortia lacked—and only much later did it become clear how great a weakness it was—was an advocate of the calibre of Hinton at the CEGB and Sir William Penney at the UK AEA. These two monopoly organisations had no great liking for each other's views but, in a kind of conspiracy that occurs from time to time in the British system of 'government by stealth', they preferred to work for an agreed decision rather than have one dictated by the consortia for which they shared something akin to contempt. The one man who might have stood up successfully to the 'conspirators', Sir Claud Gibb of Parsons, chairman of the Nuclear Power Plant Company, had been killed in an aircrash in 1959.

The outcome was that, although the CEGB set up an 'assessment' to decide on the choice of reactor for a new nuclear station at Dungeness in Kent, the outcome in reality was pre-ordained. The Labour government of 1964 had already indicated to the CEGB that a decision for anything but the AGR would be over-ruled. The con-

sortia unwittingly made the decision much easier, however, by putting what, by us reckoning at least, was a fairly high construction
price on their bids for us designs of light water reactors.

Dungeness B

Although no one recognised it at the time, the Dungeness B appraisal
in 1965 marked the beginning of the end of the consortia system for
nuclear station construction in Britain. By 1972 the CEGB was
acknowledging that its clumsy attempts to secure benefits by insisting
on competition between rival consortia had increased rather than
reduced the cost of its nuclear stations. It was also wondering whether
it would ever see any power from Dungeness B.

The outcome of the Dungeness B assessment was the awarding of
a £79 million contract to Atomic Power Construction, the consortium which in 1963 had been crippled when it failed to secure the
second Wylfa reactor and then left for dead when GEC, its chief
shareholder, pulled out. But the UK AEA engineers, recognising the
strong predilection of the other two consortia for us technology
(although both were also tendering AGR designs), approached APC,
which had no plans of its own to tender. They suggested how, by
re-arranging the fuel in a more compact way, the core of the AGR
would produce 20 per cent more power. As a result APC entered a
hasty bid that offered electricity from an AGR for a lusty 10 per cent
less than fossil-fuelled stations, and a still greater advantage over us
water reactors.

No one at the time seemed unduly perturbed that the CEGB should
be putting so much faith in the smallest and weakest of the under-
nourished nuclear consortia. Some fairly senior UK AEA staff who had
worked on the 33MW prototype AGR at Windscale were induced to
join APC, though they included no one of the rank of those who had
actually participated in the assessment. But the inadequacies of the
entire consortia system and its relationship with the customer and research agency, already clearly apparent in the magnox programme,
were vastly amplified by Dungeness B. Where the magnox programme
began by building reactors not much more than twice the size of the
50MW reactors of Calder Hall, Dungeness B's 625MW reactors meant
a scale-up factor of nearly twenty. Gas pressure was twice as high,
and the fuel arrangement had been radically revised to improve the
reactor rating.

Just how little effort had gone into the design when the contract
was placed in 1966, and how far short of the task fell the consortium's
effort thereafter, was all too clearly apparent by 1970—the year the
first reactor was scheduled to produce power. That year the station

was still an estimated five years from completion. Design errors and mismanagement of fairly straightforward parts of the construction had almost brought work to a halt. The consortium itself had come to an end, its two shareholding companies brought to the verge of bankruptcy by the CEGB. One of the remaining two consortia had accepted the task of managing the project and trying to get it back on course. By 1974 the most optimistic estimate for first power from Dungeness B was 1976–7. Cost was expected to exceed £250 million —three times the winning bid of 1964.

Long and costly road

To put Dungeness B into perspective, however, before we consider the fate of the rest of Britain's second nuclear power programme, let us look briefly abroad. Britain has not been alone in its nuclear power troubles. All those nations which pioneered the peaceful use of the atom have found it a complex, frustrating and immensely costly operation. France, which followed a course very similar to Britain's for its first generation of nuclear stations, failed to develop a successor and turned instead to US water reactors. Sweden erred in the physics of one nuclear system, and had to complete its Marviken station as a conventional oil-fired station. The Canadians got into deep trouble with both their prototype Candu reactor at Douglas Point and with heavy water supplies, before breaking through in the 1970s with one of the world's most successful nuclear stations, the 2,000MW Pickering plant near Toronto. US General Electric admitted in 1974 that a fuel reprocessing plant it had built at Morris, near Chicago, would not work, and would take four years and an estimated $90–130 million to rebuild.

But the nuclear plant that obliged the CEGB to take seriously the possibility of a foreign reactor for its second nuclear power programme was Oyster Creek, which US General Electric succeeded in selling the US utility Jersey Central Power and Light late in 1964. This was the commercial breakthrough for the US reactor vendors; the first order for the big new light water reactors, which were in effect the second generation of the light water reactors. By 1971 the customer was suing the vendor for $62·5 million.

US General Electric had offered to build the complete 500MW station at a fixed price, with completion scheduled for 1967. Similar offers were made at this time to the CEGB. They were too attractive— superficially at least—to ignore. In the event Oyster Creek was more than two years late coming on-load, and even then took many months to reach full power. It lost a great deal of money for the vendor 'because of soaring construction costs, changes in licensing

requirements during construction and other problems'. Dr. Thomas
O. Paine, the man who was directing NASA when men first landed on
the moon but who later returned to US General Electric to head its
$2,000 million a year power division, admits that Oyster Creek over-
shot its estimated cost by more than 50 per cent. What is more, he
expected US General Electric to lose money on every one of the first
eleven big nuclear contracts it had landed.

'With Oyster Creek we grasped the nettle,' he told me in an interview in 1971, when we discussed how the US had launched its nuclear
programme.[1] The company not only guaranteed full output but also
promised that it would 'stretch' from 500 to 600MW output; and,
although safety regulations were made much tougher during construction, the station has achieved its 'stretched' rating. The losses
on those first eleven stations were part of the price US General Electric
was prepared to pay as 'entrance fee' to the nuclear business. When
Royal Dutch Shell in 1973 decided to buy its way into the business
in a joint nuclear venture with Gulf Oil, the 'entrance fee' was $200
million. A year later it had made provision for possible losses of
another $250 million on the ten nuclear reactors the joint venture,
General Atomic, then had on its order book. Figures published in the
US business journal *Forbes* early in 1969 indicated that the four US
nuclear vendors marketing light water reactors had already spent a
total of more than $500m. of their shareholders' money, of which the
biggest single stake was $200 million invested by US General Electric.[2]
None of the British nuclear consortia in the late 1960s could even
contemplate sums of this magnitude. In Britain the financial burden
fell squarely upon the customers, namely, the generating boards
and particularly the CEGB.

Design your way out

The imbalance of talent between, on the one hand, research and
development and, on the other, detailed design and manufacture is,
I believe, the root cause of the troubles of Britain's nuclear industry.
On one side there were two powerful organisations dedicated to
technological progress in the belief that:

$$\text{bigger} + \text{hotter} = \text{more efficient} + \text{cheaper}.$$

The formula is in accord with the laws of physics and economics.
Where it falls down is when the scientists and engineers underestimate the problems 'bigger + hotter' can bring in its wake for an

[1] By the end of 1973 orders had been placed by US utilities for 214 nuclear stations,
totalling more than 200,000MW.
[2] *Forbes*, 1 February 1969, pp. 30–2.

industry already struggling with the novelty and complexity of nuclear power. The same industry hit precisely the same kind of problems when the customer attempted to stretch designs of boilers and turbo-generators. To take turbo-generators, for example, what the customer believed was no more than an extrapolation of well-proven 275mw machines to 500mw sizes invoked unforeseen problems that will mean the 500mw machines will probably never run at their full design rating. *Table 4* charts the CEGB's experience during the 1960s in developing the 500mw machines.

It is noteworthy that the nations which have done best at harnessing the atom are Germany and Japan, both of which entered the nuclear industry 'downstream', by investing in US technology and concentrating on using it as efficiently as possible. The Japanese have even completed a nuclear station in under four years, while elsewhere construction times range from five to ten years.

Perpetual pressure to advance the technology—to design your way out of your problems—creates its own vicious circle. The cost of learning new techniques and ironing out troubles can more than offset any economic advantage, further increasing the pressure to find something better. By 1969 the CEGB, only four years after taking its decision to buy AGRs and still several years from obtaining any power, was publicly discussing the introduction of a third generation of gas-cooled reactors. Once more there was confident talk from the CEGB of extrapolating experience gleaned from the first two generations to a still hotter, more compact reactor, called the high-temperature reactor. Once again the CEGB had completely missed the real issue: that what the industry desperately needed was some genuine assistance in capitalising on experience already gained. The CEGB persisted—against all the evidence—in believing that by pitting the feeble British nuclear consortia against one another it was getting the best possible commercial deal for the electricity consumer.

Turning point

The summer of 1972 was a turning point for the starved and beaten British nuclear industry. Early that year Lord Robens's autobiography of his ten years with the Coal Board had been published. In a chapter called 'Nuclear Scandals' that showed scant concern for objectivity or facts, he wrote: 'there is even now still no nuclear power station producing electricity within 25 per cent as cheaply as that being sent out from the modern coal-fired stations based on the coalfields'.[1] Sir Stanley Brown, who had succeeded Hinton in 1965 as chairman of the CEGB, but whose own retirement was fast approach-

[1] Lord Robens, *Ten Year Stint*, Cassell, 1972, pp. 178–205.

ing, was infuriated by the inaccuracies and personal innuendo. He took the unprecedented step of releasing to the Press a table of the three most efficient coal, oil and nuclear stations in its system. Rising costs of coal and oil, together with greatly increased construction costs that were by no means confined to nuclear plant, had turned the tables on coal. The cheapest electricity in the CEGB's system was being generated by nuclear stations with the best coal-fired station running a poor third. The trend was confirmed in 1974, when the CEGB updated its league table (*table 5*).

In mid-summer 1972 Brown was succeeded by Mr. Arthur Hawkins, a man whose experience was very different from the eminent engineers who had dominated the CEGB for fifteen years from its birth in 1957. The government had clearly decided it was time for a change and gave the post to an operations man. Swiftly the Board took on a completely new cast, dedicated to getting better

	Reactor	Origins	Principal commercial vendors (1)		Fuel		Safety		Manufacture	
British Reactors	Magnox	UK nuclear weapons programme	National Nuclear Corporation	B	Natural uranium	A	Acceptable to U.K.	A	UK has the experience	A
	Advanced Gas-cooled Reactor (AGR)	Uprated version of Magnox	National Nuclear Corporation	B	Enriched uranium	A	Acceptable to UK	A	UK has bought experience dearly (5)	B
	High-Temperature Reactor (HTR)	Development of Gas-cooled Reactor	Nat. Nuclear Corporation +Gen. Atomic (Shell/Gulf joint venture)	B	Enriched uranium (2)	B	Acceptable to UK	A	Untried but believed simpler than AGR (5)	B
	Steam-Generating Heavy Water Reactor (SGHWR)	Insurance policy against hitch in AGR project	Nat. Nuclear Corporation +Atomic Energy of Canada	B	Enriched uranium	A	Acceptable to UK	A	Straight-forward— mostly factory built	A
Foreign Reactors	CANDU (Canada)	Canadian domestic nuclear power project	Atomic Energy of Canada	B	Natural uranium (3)	B	Acceptable to UK	A	Straight-forward— mostly factory built (3)	A
	Boiling Water Reactor (BWR)	US military submarine project	US General Electric or Babcock & Wilcox	B	Enriched uranium	A	Not yet accepted in UK (4)	B	Untried in UK (6)	B
	Pressurised Water Reactor (PWR)	US military submarine project	Westinghouse Electric or Combustion Engineering or Babcock & Wilcox	B	Enriched uranium	A	Not yet accepted in UK (4)	B	Untried in UK (6)	B

KEY:

A—*No obvious problems*
B—*Some problems*
C—*Serious problems*

(1) All vendors untried in new UK circumstances.
(2) Still some doubts about large-scale manufacture of fuel.
(3) Substitutes enriched (heavy) water for enriched uranium, and some worries still about adequate supplies.
(4) Proposals for this system could still be rejected outright by the chief nuclear inspector, or major modifications demanded that would require a new design.
(5) Acceptable designs still not ready.
(6) Sufficiently novel to UK experience, especially in pressure vessel and steam generator, to raise significant doubts.

Figure 3 Comparison of seven thermal nuclear reactor systems.

performance from established practice instead of trying to squeeze the last ounce of efficiency from an advancing technology.

Then in August 1972 the government finally decided that the consortia system, sustained for so long largely at the insistence of the CEGB, must be abandoned. It declared its intention of creating instead a 'single strong unit' to build the combination of reactor and boilers known as the nuclear steam supply system for future British nuclear power stations.[1] The generating boards themselves would order separately the 'balance of plant', namely as turbo-generators, switchgear, and so on. Which reactors the new British nuclear company would be building, however, could not yet be decided. On the conclusion reached by the Vinter committee, which I mentioned at the start of this chapter, the government needed another eighteen months before it could take this decision. By then,

Export potential		Costs (8)				Commercial risk		Comment	Overall rating
		Capital		Generating					
Probably Nil	C	High	C	Average	B	Low—though New design needed	A	5,000 MW installed at about 25% above original estimate	B +
Probably Nil (7)	C	Average	B	Average	A	Greater than Magnox— new design needed (10)	B	6,000 under construction, at estimated 100% above original estimate	B +
Beginning to look very Encouraging	A	Average	B	Average	A	Significant (11)	B	Contracts for 10,000 MW placed or being negotiated in the US	B +
Encouraging	B	Average	B	Average	A	Low (9)	A	100 MW prototype only	A −
Beginning to look very Encouraging	A	High	B	Low	A	Low	A	2,200 MW operating in Canada 12,000 MW under construction or planned	A −
Very Encouraging	A	Low	A	Low	A	New design may be needed to satisfy safety (12)	B	9,500 MW operating in US	B +
Very Encouraging	A	Low	A	Low	A	New design may be needed to satisfy safety (12)	B	15,000 MW operating in US	B +

(7) Probably a realistic assessment, though Japan is still interested.
(8) CEGB acknowledges that all reactors except Magnox are in the same 'ballpark' on generation costs. Industry questions the very low capital costs claimed for BWR and PWR, based on US estimates.
(9) Based on recent experience of similar CANDU system.
(10) Generating Boards are worried about major features of present AGR design, notably hot dome and insulation.
(11) Generating Boards say this system is not yet ready for series ordering.
(12) In CEGB view, a major redesign would rule out this reactor.

[1] The *Financial Times*, 9 August 1972.

it was hoped, the first AGR would be operating and much more information would be available about rival British and foreign systems.

The 'single strong unit'

Painfully slowly throughout 1973 the form and structure of the new nuclear company took shape. The first step, early in 1973, was the government's announcement that it would be a £10 million company in which the General Electric Company would take a 50 per cent stake and play the dominant role.[1] The 'strong man' the industry had lacked since the death of Sir Claud Gibb was to be Sir Arnold Weinstock, chief executive of GEC, which had been transformed under his leadership during the 1960s into one of Britain's biggest and financially strongest organisations. The government itself would have 15 per cent of the new company, through its research agency the UK AEA, spending over £40 million a year on reactor R & D. The balance of 35 per cent would be held by private industry. Not until late in the year, however, did private industry decide how the 35 per cent was to be apportioned. It would be shared among seven of the eight remaining private shareholders of what once had been five nuclear consortia. Only one company—Parsons—declined, while others outside the consortia were turned away. The government's decision had passed its first big test—it had the confidence of the great majority of the nuclear industry.

But in creating its single strong unit the government knew it was courting fresh risks. If the company was to be strong enough to enter into an equitable customer–contractor relationship with the CEGB, might there not be a danger of decisions that ignored wider national interests? An example might be a decision on the choice of reactor that in the longer term might leave British nuclear power policy effectively in the control of another nation. The growing demands of the Arab nations were already alerting the nation to such a risk. Another example might be a decision that so inflamed public fears about nuclear safety that it severely embarrassed the government. A third might be a decision with significant short- or long-term implications for the balance of payments. The government's answer was to create a Nuclear Power Advisory Board of top-level officials to advise it on major questions of nuclear power strategy. The Secretary of State for Trade and Industry, Mr. Peter Walker, who set up the NPAB, soon decided that he himself would be its chairman.[2] Its

[1] David Fishlock, 'The priority of questions in nuclear power', the *Financial Times*, 23 March 1973.
[2] Departmental responsibility passed to the newly created Secretary of State for Energy early in 1974, when Lord Carrington became the NPAB's chairman; later to be replaced by Mr. Eric Varley of the new Labour government of February 1974.

great merit soon became clear, in that it forced people to back with hard facts—and above all with their own reputations—views that previously they had been expressing promiscuously in private and, what is more, changing almost as freely.

Late in 1973 the NPAB began to wrestle with the overridingly important question at that stage of the choice of reactor (*see figure 3* for the contenders). It had before it the conclusions of Vinter's committee made eighteen months before, that there were drawbacks to all four possible choices of British reactor, but none so serious that it disqualified the system. In such circumstances the advantage would lie with the reactor already under construction—except that here there was general agreement that no more AGRs should be ordered until at least one was working. Completion date for the first AGR was still receding, from late 1973 to the spring or even the summer of 1974. What was worse, Britain had repeated one of the most serious objections to its magnox programme. Once again it was building not one AGR design but three very different ones, each effectively a prototype. And if another were ordered, experience had taught that it should be both much larger and quite significantly different from any under construction. In short, it had to be a fourth prototype.

In the truest traditions of decision-making in Britain, the government decreed that the deliberations of the NPAB should be kept secret. In the case of the reactor choice the government itself would announce its decision on the next reactor the CEGB would order. But it was not to be. For a start, Hawkins, an autocrat accustomed to taking a decision and driving it through, had no liking for the idea of a dictated choice. He had already indicated a preference for importing US reactor technology. He thus disclosed that, with the backing of a major US nuclear vendor, he believed the National Nuclear Corporation, Britain's new single strong unit, could build light water reactors on time and to the quoted price and performance.[1]

Reaching a decision

Lord Aldington, chairman of the National Nuclear Corporation and a man with long experience both in parliament and in energy politics, remarked to me a few weeks before the government announced its decision that 'not in my wildest days in politics have I known any decision so confounded by falsehoods'. Battle was joined on the eve of the NPAB's first meeting in November 1973, when the CEGB released 'unattributably' to the Press its case for buying the US pressur-

[1] David Fishlock, the *Financial Times*, 12 September 1973.

ised water reactor. Its case was that so imperative was it that Britain should begin to bring a lot of new nuclear power into service in the early 1980s, it must choose a reactor that needed no further development and would need no significant modifications to conform with British requirements. The only reactor that satisfied these demands was a Westinghouse design of 1,200MW pressurised water reactor. Given the reactor of its choice, however, the CEGB was ready to order a very large amount of new nuclear power in the near future. The idea was enticing to an industry that had not had a new nuclear order for over three years. But it raised huge questions for government. What risks might be hidden in placing so much faith in foreign energy technology? Was the US reactor safe enough for a small, overcrowded island? Was the CEGB's choice really the answer to poor performance by the British plant construction industry that seemed to afflict *all* types of power stations and many other large projects? Were alternative British reactor designs really as bad as the CEGB was implying? Would Britain ever see power from a £600 million investment in AGRS?

What finally flushed the whole debate into the public arena was the decision of the Parliamentary Select Committee on Science and Technology to hold a hasty inquiry. It called six witnesses, all key figures in the reactor decision. Arthur Hawkins, Frank Tombs (chairman of the South of Scotland Generating Board) and Sir John Hill (chairman of the UK AEA) and Lord Aldington were all members of the NPAB. Sir Arnold Weinstock, managing director of GEC, was generally acknowledged to be the man who would 'call the shots' in the National Nuclear Corporation. The sixth man—in some respects the most important of all—was Mr. E. C. (Bill) Williams, the government's chief nuclear inspector.

The evidence of the six showed that, far from being a clear-cut decision as the CEGB proposition implied, reactor choice was still a wide-open question.[1] Far from being convinced by the 'logic' of the CEGB's case, some members of the NPAB were in strong disagreement. Neither were they alone in condemning Hawkins' attempt to force the government's hand. Williams, moreover, assured the MPs there had been 'no detailed discussions' of the safety aspects of the CEGB's plans and that he had 'no way of inferring where they got their confidence from'. By no stretch of the imagination could the Select Committee's inquiry be called impartial. Its object was simply and solely to try to persuade the government to reject the CEGB's plan to import US reactor technology. Whether it had any more influence here than it had in an earlier equally partisan inquiry into Tracked

[1] Report of the Select Committee on Science and Technology, February 1974.

Hovercraft (*see chapter 6*) is not easily judged. But the fact remains that it brought into the open the basis for a decision which otherwise may never have been made public.

'The steamer' is chosen

Four years of uncertainty and acrimonious debate ended officially on 10 July 1974, when energy secretary Eric Varley announced a 'very firm and positive committment' to the steam generating heavy water reactor (SGHWR).[1] This was a British-designed water reactor, conceived in the early 1960s as an insurance policy lest something unexpected should impede the gas-cooled reactor developments in Britain. In the words of one UK AEA executive, it 'was for once a reactor born of intellect, not of expediency'. Its designers first combed the world for ideas on water reactors, and combined some of the best in their design. Above all they sought a design that would minimise the amount of engineering work needed on site—one of the great weaknesses, as it turned out, of the AGR programme.

A large prototype steamer of 100MW was built on schedule by the UK AEA, at a cost slightly less than was estimated (*see figure 9*)—an almost unprecedented event in high technology. Altogether about £90 million had been invested in designing, building and operating the prototype and in commercial component and fuel development when the decision was taken.

Mr. Varley cited six reasons for choosing the steamer: that it would provide power reliably, could be ordered quickly, should meet no safety objections, offered particular scope for British technology, and was backed by six years of successful operation of the prototype and by Canadian experience with the similar Candu system (from which, incidentally, some of its best features had been drawn).

But the government's commitment was for only a modest 4,000MW of power from the steamer—a pilot programme, in fact, that would give the industry just enough incentive to take the decision seriously and lay a sound manufacturing base for expansion later. The orders were expected to be for six 660MW reactors, substantially similar to the prototype reactor and only six times its size.

Thus the government totally rejected the CEGB's case not only for ordering 1,200MW Westinghouse PWRs, but that, given the reactor of its choice, it would be needing some 36,000MW of nuclear power over the decade 1973–83. It therefore sacrificed what Sir Arnold Weinstock believed was the strongest card of all—his plan for uniting the National Nuclear Corporation with Westinghouse and the French

[1] David Fishlock, 'Varley comes out in favour of British designed reactors', the *Financial Times*, 11 July 1974.

C

nuclear industry in a powerful tripartite 'club' dominating reactor design and construction in Europe. He expressed his disapproval of the decision by asking the government to reduce GEC's shareholding in the National Nuclear Corporation.

Two factors—both unacceptable to the government—probably account for the large disparity between CEGB estimates and the government nuclear programme. One is that the CEGB simply took an unduly optimistic view of the growth in demand for its own product in an era of fast-rising energy costs, and refused to modify its estimates even when the consequences of political action by Arab oil-producers became apparent. The other is that the CEGB was seeking to reduce as quickly as possible its dependence of fossil fuels, particularly coal, and was prepared to greatly increase its margin of surplus generating capacity in order to achieve flexibility and hence greater control of fuel costs.

The government's decision, although confidently anticipated by the *Financial Times* eleven weeks before it was officially announced,[1] apparently came as a stunning blow to the CEGB. It was undoubtedly the least prepared of all interested parties to implement the decision, because it had closed its mind to any alternative to the reactor of its choice.[2] There is an elegant theory to account for the CEGB's single-minded concentration on a solution to its own technical and commercial problems to the exclusion of a host of political factors, from coal industry pressures to public concern for nuclear safety. Briefly it argues that, so formidable is the problem of operating a nationwide machine to keep the wildly fluctuating demands of consumers supplied with a product that cannot be stored, that the industry rarely raises its sights from its control panels. In other words, its basic fault is not so much the arrogance of which it is often accused but simply dedication to duty. Nonetheless it is a serious flaw and government, nuclear industry and consumers are all watching closely to see how it reacts to a rude but perhaps very salutary shock.

[1] David Fishlock, "Next reactor likely to be UK-designed", the *Financial Times*, 25 April 1974.
[2] David Fishlock, 'The changes needed to make a success of "the steamer"', the *Financial Times*, 31 July 1974.

Table 4 Development of 500mw turbogenerators in uk: 8 years from concept to full rating

Late 1959	First work on design of 500mw unit by extrapolation from design of existing 200mw units.
May 1960	Issue of first inquiry by cegb to manufacturers.
Jan. 1961	First order: 4 × 500mw units for West Burton station.
Sept. 1966	First 500mw unit synchronised.
Aug. 1967	Nameplate rating of first unit achieved.
Oct. 1973	Total of 42 500mw units installed.

Table 5 Production costs of cegb power stations supplying the national grid (including operating costs and capital charges on construction costs)

		Pence per kWh	
		1972–73	1971
Dungeness A	Nuclear	0·33	0·31
Pembroke	Oil	0·39	0·38
Fawley	Oil	0·39	0·41
Ferrybridge c	Coal	0·40	0·36
Sizewell	Nuclear	0·40	0·32
Ratcliffe ⎱	Coal	0·41	0·35
Oldbury ⎰	Nuclear	0·41	0·38
Eggborough	Coal	0·42	0·37
Kingsnorth	Oil	0·43	0·36

CHAPTER 5

The business of science

'What fun it would be to spend life doing cosmology at the taxpayer's expense,' remarked Dr. Ieuan Maddock one day over lunch at the *Financial Times*.

Maddock, a physicist and Fellow of the Royal Society, who played a key part in the development of Britain's nuclear armoury, has spent the past decade wrestling with the administration of science for a large ministry, the Department of Trade and Industry (formerly the Ministry of Technology). Professor Sir Hermann Bondi FRS, his opposite number as chief scientific adviser to the Ministry of Defence, does find some spare time for cosmology. He is professor of mathematics at King's College, just a few hundred yards along the Embankment from his office in Whitehall, and has an international reputation for his science. But mostly his time is spent administering the £50 million a year his government department spends on 'untargeted' research—from which comes many of the best ideas for new military equipment—and advising on a total defence research and development budget exceeding £400 million.

Another top British science administrator who resolutely makes time for his own research is Walter Marshall FRS, responsible for the £25 million a year research programme of the UK Atomic Energy Authority, in addition to being chief scientist at the Department of Energy. When in the late 1960s Dr. Marshall shouldered the task of reversing the trend of the huge Harwell laboratory (5,000 staff) to drift deep into the academic reaches of science, he made it a condition that he himself should spend a few weeks away from Harwell each year doing research in solid-state physics. If he failed—and his 'commercial' plans for Harwell, as we shall see in chapter 9, had plenty of opposition among scientists as well as among his prospective customers in industry—his own reputation as a scientist would remain intact. As he has shown by published papers year by year, Marshall still has much to contribute to his own science.

Walter Marshall, now in his early forties, has no illusions about which is the easier way of life. In the heat of battle he has all too little time to worry about the very large number of decisions he is asked to take on the fate of research projects and the future of scientists whose proclivities and problems he understands so well. But each year when he returns to Harwell from his brief 'sabbatical' in some national research centre abroad, it is brought home just how much harder he works at the business of science than at science itself.

If a creative man wants to spend his life painting or writing music or history, he seeks a patron—the state or a private sponsor—and if he is lucky he gets paid a few hundred or a few thousand pounds a year to pursue his main interest in life. This is so for the scientist too —except for one thing. The scientist today tends to need a huge infrastructure of apparatus, computing power and supporting staff to make any headway. No longer is science simply a commitment on the patron's part to back one man and his creative talent. The patron must now provide an infrastructure that can cost several times, sometimes many times, the scientist's own livelihood to maintain.

For the patron this raises a new kind of problem. Not only has he to pick the outstanding talent to back—for the difference between good talent and an outstanding talent in science is an immensely large factor in terms of achievement—but so large is the investment that he has to find a talent that can manage his research effort in an effective yet sympathetic way. To be sympathetic the manager has to be a scientist whose own research achievements command the respect of the staff. To be effective he has to be first and foremost a man who can manage.

Scientists generally, anarchists as most of them are at heart, have not shown themselves overly sympathetic to their patrons' problems. They were pleased to find themselves after the Second World War in favour with a public persuaded that, if simply left to their own devices, they would produce answers in their own time to society's more intractable problems. But they resented any attempt by the patron to channel their cogitations towards one of those problems. They saw themselves participating in what essentially was a cultural pursuit. Their attitude seemed to be, if the patron had a problem to solve, then he should recruit lesser mortals for the task.

The high-energy physicists illustrate my point well. Their interest lies at the boundaries of our knowledge of physics, far from any conceivable application. They readily recognised the significance of major wartime developments in the 'calutrons' and in radar developments for their own ambitions. Those ambitions are to dissect matter more and more finely until they arrive at the ultimate 'building blocks'. It was—and still is—one of the scientifically most exciting sectors of exploration; an intellectual challenge attractive to many of the most fertile minds of science.

The basic tool of their trade is the 'atom-smasher', a novel kind of dissecting microscope that enabled these scientists to fragment nuclei of atoms in such a way that they could follow the paths, properties and ultimate fate of each fragment.

Now it is an unfortunate but unsurmountable law of physics that the finer the fragments, the more powerful the machines you must employ. No one could tell how much energy it would take to arrive at the 'building blocks' but the physicists could foresee many years of learning to build machines of ever-increasing energy and expense before they reached their goal.

They prepared their ground well. They had only to hint to the politicians that their quest for an understanding of the nature of matter might hold clues of crucial importance—perhaps a new energy source to tap—for governments to spend freely on high-energy physics. Atom smashing now needs the world's largest machines. The latest, under construction near Geneva, is being buried in a sub-terranean tunnel 2·2 kilometres in diameter beneath French farm-land. Its cost by 1976 will have exceeded £120 million.

Britain's share of the capital cost of this European collaboration in high-energy physics, some £25 million, is administered by the Science Research Council, a body of rigorous standards of excellence in the science it will support. Chairman of the Science Research Council for six critical years, 1967–73, was Professor Sir Brian Flowers, a solid-state physicist with a Chair at Manchester and a flair for administer-ing research.[1] Flowers found two things very seriously awry at the Science Research Council in 1966. The first was that although the science—predominantly physics and chemistry—his council was supporting to the tune of £34 million a year in 1966 was the science underlying many of the objectives of the (then) Ministry of Techno-logy, almost no communication existed between his council and the ministry. Flowers energetically set about building bridges between the two. Without relaxing his council's standards on the scientific quality of the proposals he accepted, he supported projects and pro-grammes of direct relevance to the ministry's aspirations. As we shall see later, his foresight stood him in very good stead when Lord Rothschild came up with his 'customer–contractor relationship'.

The second flaw Flowers found was the size of his council's commit-ment to high-energy physics. In 1966–7 it was absorbing 45 per cent of the budget. Not only was it committed to finding some 20 per cent of the budget of CERN, the European research centre near Geneva, but it was operating two national laboratories, Rutherford and Daresbury, each with its own atom smasher. The heavy commitments in staff and resources these great machines command imply a power-

[1] Sir Brian Flowers is now rector of Imperial College, London.

ful resistance to change. Moreover, there were plans afoot, as we shall see in chapter 6, to fund a still more expensive machine for CERN.

By an adroit act of juggling Flowers succeeded in giving the high-energy physicists funds for their new machine at CERN while reducing the proportion of the Science Research Council's budget absorbed by this branch of science, from 45 per cent to 41 per cent by 1972–3.

The fate of FREDY

It takes a great deal of courage and patience to achieve what Flowers achieved in six years of dealing with the prima donnas of British science. Walter Marshall once told a gathering of US scientists that he had 'frequently been astonished by the way in which scientists will abandon their trained critical powers as soon as they stop talking about purely scientific matters'. Such was certainly the case when early in 1972 Flowers decided to question the cash he was spending on a new branch of science, artificial intelligence, and specifically on a project called FREDY. From modest beginnings in Britain early in the 1960s, this science had begun to enlarge its requests for financial support at a rather alarming rate. What Flowers had to decide was whether the progress artificial intelligence was making, or looked like making, could justify greatly increased support. Not least of his problems was the conflicting and emotion-laden advice he was getting from the leading scientists in the field.

Artificial intelligence can be defined as the experimental study of cognitive activity in the abstract. It extends from studies of human or animal thought processes to machines that attempt to simulate a brain. Public interest in artificial intelligence has focused almost exclusively on these simulations—that is, on robots—a point its practitioners have not been slow to exploit.

Britain's biggest and best-known university department in the field is the School of Artificial Intelligence at the University of Edinburgh. Since 1963 Professor Donald Michie, a geneticist of puckish appearance and humour, has led a group studying that facet of computer science popularly known as robotics. Michie's early efforts to teach the computer to play chess soon earned him popular acclaim.

Partly because it has attracted public attention and partly because (once some pretty basic questions have been answered) it could point the way to much more powerful computers, robotics today is a fashionable area of scientific research. This is especially so in the US, where a big effort is maintained by such institutions as MIT and the University of Stanford, but Japan and Russia have also taken great interest.

At roughly £100,000 a year plus the services of a powerful computer, artificial intelligence was *per capita* one of the most expensive research activities supported by the Science Research Council. Most of this money, moreover, was going to Michie's group, whose robot when 'thinking' monopolised the entire capacity of the ICL 4130 computer. Then Michie put in requests for much bigger funds—proposals which at one stage totalled about £2 million, including the cost of a more advanced computer. It was time, the Science Research Council decided, to ask the crucial question: Did the progress Michie was making warrant further support?

At Edinburgh, Donald Michie had a colleague and one-time close associate of high academic reputation, Professor H. C. Longuet-Higgins, leading a group in theoretical psychology in the School of Artificial Intelligence. But a rift had developed between the two scientists and the highly influential Longuet-Higgins was now strongly advising the council that it would be wasting its funds by putting more effort into robotics before more had been learned about the mechanism of biological intelligence. Thus it was that the embryonic science of artificial intelligence in Britain in the 1970s became polarised between these two conflicting viewpoints—those supporting Michie and his glamorous robots and those supporting Longuet-Higgins and his more austere arguments for better theories first.

Flowers first attempted to break the deadlock in a time-honoured fashion—by calling in a distinguished outsider to arbitrate. He persuaded Sir James Lighthill, Lucerian Professor of Mathematics at Cambridge, to take on the task of deciding whether more funds should be allocated to artificial intelligence. Lighthill's report was both ingenious and damning. He had the temerity to attempt to make his own classification of the various aspects of research on artificial intelligence—a move that was bound to infuriate any 'insider' who disagreed with his conclusions. Those conclusions were broadly that bigger and better robots, such as Michie was advocating, did not look a promising way of gaining a better understanding of 'intelligence', but the application of robots in engineering should have a better chance of success.

The Lighthill report caused a great storm in the field of artificial intelligence. For Flowers it raised more questions than it answered, so strong were the objections to Lighthill's classification, on which his conclusions were founded. Flowers set the report to one side[1] and tried another approach, also time-honoured among scientists. He asked a special panel of scientists knowledgeable of artificial intelligence—his peers so to speak—to investigate Michie's work. This

[1] But see *Artificial Intelligence*, published by the Science Research Council, April 1973.

'grant monitoring panel' gave Michie a challenge: choose your own yardstick to convince us that your robot behaves intelligently. Michie accepted, and in February 1973 the panel assembled in Edinburgh to watch FREDY perform.

FREDY is a machine that can take a heap of seven wooden bricks— a body, two axles, four wheels—sort them out and assemble them into a model car. Then with a final flourish it gives the model a gentle shove to make sure that all of its wheels are working. The question was whether, in assembling its toy, FREDY was behaving intelligently or whether the whole process was merely a sophisticated extension of the sort of pre-programmed automatic assembly operations the motorcar and other industries use every day.

Sadly, the panel found that FREDY was really rather dim; that the process was conventional computer programming of a very competent nature but not true artificial intelligence. In short, Michie and his group had not achieved what they had set out to do, and been financed to do. To persevere with robots, the panel concluded, was not a good use of the Science Research Council's resources until new ideas opened up new avenues to explore.

Inevitably the group was deeply offended, not only because its main source of funds was being withdrawn but because the panel's conclusion gravely affected its standing with other groups in artificial intelligence round the world. At first Michie made the mistake of trying to argue that Britain was opting out of a field acknowledged to be important by the growing interest in robotics not just among academic institutions, but among major electronics companies round the world. His error was that he was confusing the question of importance with the merits of his own proposals; it was these that the panel had been assessing.

It is an error which, as we shall see in the next chapter, is not uncommon among scientists and engineers.

I have related the downfall of FREDY at length because it illustrates three important points about the management and control of scientists:

1. The difficulty of stopping a research project.
2. The readiness with which scientists will abandon their training once they venture beyond the narrow confines of their discipline—into the politics of research finance, for example.
3. The basic difference between pure and applied science.

The first two points recur in examples I give in subsequent chapters. The third point was made clearly when Michie, frustrated in his efforts to obtain Science Research Council support for his studies of 'cognitive activity in the abstract', promptly set about redrafting his proposals with a view to securing contracts and grants for the application of the robot FREDY and the ideas he embodied to practical engineering situations. This, incidentally, was the way most of the other research groups in artificial intelligence were tending to go. All had hit the same problems in advancing their understanding of intelligence, but all recognised that their robots embodied techniques engineering could well use.

Who needs science?

If any scientist is naïve enough to believe that science these days is all (or even mainly) about the pursuit of knowledge for its own sake, he should spend a while browsing through a thick book of the statistics of research published in 1973 by the Central Statistical Office.[1] This book records the way in which Britain spent £10,000 million on science in the 1960s—who donated it and how it was spent. He would discover that industry—private, public and overseas—provided about half the cash (*figure 4*). It did not do so for any altruistic motive but because it thought scientists could help solve its problems —by inventing new products or showing how to make the old ones quicker, cheaper or better, and how to clean up any mess it might make along the way. The solution, of course, can lie anywhere between a new physical effect and fresh insight into human behaviour.

Government provides the other half of the cash (*figure 4*). It does so for reasons basically similar to those of commerce. It also has problems—national security for one, a fiercely competitive business with every nation seeking ingenious new ways of securing its frontiers while trying to penetrate those of the others. Disease is another; while government may not see ill-health in terms of the number of pills it might sell in some disease sector, it does see it in terms of a cost to the public, any attack on which must affect value for money.

Government, however, must take a longer view of science than industry can normally afford to do. Industry rarely attempts to look more than ten years ahead, while five is far more common. The lead time on high technology, however, may well be ten years from concept to production, and longer still before peak earnings are reached. Similarly, government attempts to shoulder the problems of providing a bedrock of standards to which industry can work, and an educational system that will train new generations of problem-solvers for science.

It is within these three broad demands on government-funded science—long-range requirements, standards and education—that

[1] *Research and Development Expenditure*, HMSO, 1973.

scientists find the greatest freedom. From these three sectors come most—though not all—of the Nobel Prize winners.

The report on research and development expenditure bears another important message, however. Its scores of close-spaced tables carry the reason why Mr. Heath's government—and Mr. Wilson's before it—felt that research in Britain was getting a bit out of phase with the nation's real needs. The change both governments sought

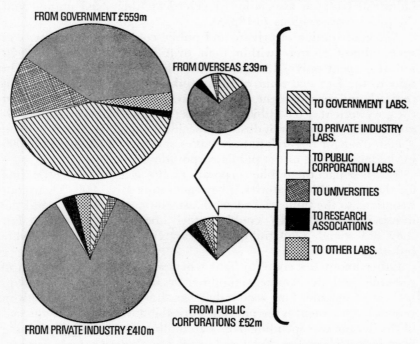

Figure 4 Where British research funds came from and where they were spent, 1969–70.

was to make scientific research in the government sector more responsive to the needs of those paying the bills, namely the taxpayers.

Down through the 1960s Britain invested a steady 2·7–2·8 per cent of its gross domestic product (GNP) in research and development. The total expanded by some 60 per cent between 1961–2 and 1969–70, from £658 million to £1,082 million. By 1973–4, the total outlay had risen to about £1,350 million.

In 1969–70 the government was British science's principal patron, providing £559 million, compared with £410 million from private industry, £52 million from the public corporations (electrical, gas, coal, steel, transport, etc.), and an income for overseas industry of £39 million. The intriguing thing about these statistics, however, is that they provide a very revealing picture of how research funds flow—and in some cases fail to flow—between different sectors of research.

The government contribution in 1969–70 was spent in roughly equal amounts in its own laboratories (£240 million) and in those of industry (£222 million). The government also provided universities and centres of higher education with £75 million for research. The industrial research associations received another £5·3 million and the public corporations £619,000.

The contribution of private and public companies, however, was spent almost entirely within their own laboratories. In 1969–70 industry spent only £13 million with the national laboratories, in spite of the fact that some of them rank in world class as centres of research and development. Industry provided only a little more than the government, £8·8 million, towards the industrial research associations which exist for industry's specific benefit. It found a mere £3·6 million for research in universities and spent a trifling £236,000 in the laboratories of the public corporations.

For their part the public corporations also seem to have little time for the national laboratories. They spent only £125,000. Their contributions to the industrial research associations (£784,000) and the universities (£600,000) could scarcely be called generous. But they did spend £8·8 million on research contracts with private industry.

Other anomalies come to light when we examine the pattern of research and development funding by industry against its main sources of income. One sector that has shown a healthy growth in research investment is the pharmaceutical industry which by the end of the decade was spending over £26 million, almost all of it coming from industry's coffers. Food and drink, too, showed a lusty increase in the 1960s, partly owing to increasing concern with product safety.

But several other industrial sectors of vital concern to Britain's overseas earnings apparently felt sufficiently sanguine about their future to allow research spending to level off and in some cases even decline. Mechanical engineering is Britain's principal source of overseas earnings. Its research budget showed a sharp increase in the mid-1960s, from £40 million to £60 million. Thereafter it remained almost static. Some of its sectors, such as machine tools and industrial plant, even declined in research investment in the late 1960s.

Over the same period, however, a contracting aerospace industry —Bristol Siddeley merged with Rolls-Royce in 1966—made increasingly heavy demands on the nation's research budget. A budget of £130 million in 1964–5 had grown to £171 million by 1969–70. Meanwhile research and development in the steel industry, most of which was nationalised in 1968, fell from nearly £13 million in 1964–5 to less than £11 million by 1969–70.

Research investment in scientific instruments was declining in the mid-1960s, then began to rise sharply from less than £11 million in 1964–5 to £17·5 million by the end of the decade. Motor vehicles increased suddenly in the mid-1960s to about £45 million but remained at this level thereafter.

In the electrical sector the research budget showed impressive growth from £107 million in 1964–5 to £187 million by the end of the decade, despite the big mergers of the late 1960s in which GEC acquired both AEI and English Electric. Precisely where the growth has taken place is not easy to say for the statistical breakdown of this sector has changed over the years. More easily spotted are sectors where there has been little growth: electrical machines (motors, transformers, turbo-generators), for example, where the spending increased only slightly from £22·5 million in 1966–7 to £25 million in 1969–70; and domestic appliances, static at about the £3 million mark throughout the latter half of the 1960s.

Commercial not cultural

In giving these figures my intention has been to emphasise one key point: that research is predominantly a business operation, financed primarily for 'commercial' and not for cultural reasons. One can easily lose sight of this point when the academics stampede, as they did when the government published its Green Paper on research late in 1971. Research as we know it nowadays is primarily a technique for solving problems (*see figure 5*): at best an astonishingly successful technique, but at worst one that can be cripplingly expensive.

No sector of research knows this better than defence research, the biggest sector of research expenditure in Britain, accounting for nearly a third of the total research and development budget (*see figure 6*). Defence research and development will cost the taxpayer £450 million in 1974–5. Most of this money will be spent in the laboratories of the industrial defence contractors, some of which maintain large 'centres of excellence' devoted exclusively to this work. But the research contracts are supported and monitored by the national defence research centres, where about a quarter of the cash is spent.

In 1971 Sir Derek Rayner, co-opted by the government from Marks and Spencer, proposed a wholesale reorganisation of the £1,000 million-a-year business of defence procurement in Britain. A key part of that reorganisation concerned the research and development function, out of which new military equipment is created.

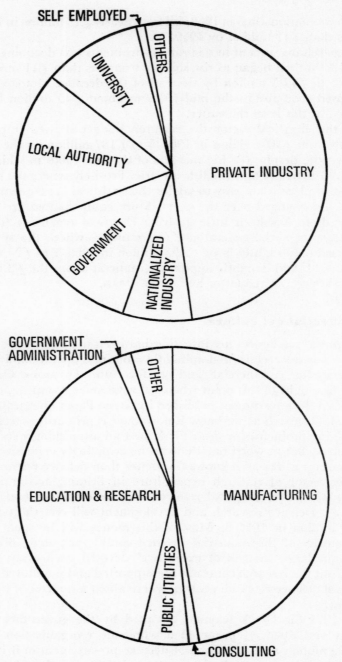

Figure 5 Who employed British scientists (above) and how they were employed, 1971.

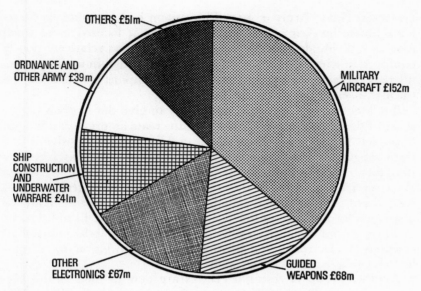

OTHERS £51m

ORDNANCE AND
OTHER ARMY £39m

MILITARY
AIRCRAFT £152m

SHIP
CONSTRUCTION
AND
UNDERWATER
WARFARE £41m

OTHER
ELECTRONICS £67m

GUIDED
WEAPONS £68m

Figure 6 UK defence 1973–4: research and development.

The change coincided with other pressures on research, such as the wave of public criticism of research in general, and specifically of the size of the defence research budget. Another heavy pressure was dissatisfaction with the way some big defence projects—such as the long-delayed Mark 24 torpedo—were being managed. A third source of sharp criticism were the defence contractors in industry, who were unhappy about the complexity of the system that monitored their contracts.

To a soft-spoken Scot, Sir George Macfarlane, as controller of defence research and development under the new Rayner procurement system, fell the daunting task of re-organising this huge research empire. Phase one of his plans will be fully implemented by the mid-1970s. The public side of these plans are a few cuts and closures, but behind the tall security fences the plans could mean a much slicker process for turning a bright idea into a deadly new weapon.

To use the current parlance of Whitehall, Macfarlane is running a contractor organisation, comprising twenty-eight research centres and test sites scattered throughout the British Isles. Their directors contract with the service chiefs to carry out research on new military projects. This idea is not new—it served as the model for Lord Rothschild's 'customer–contractor relationship' for other sectors of government science, which we shall return to in chapter 9. What is new, however, is the break with the old boundaries defining research centres as Navy, Army or RAF. This system had one obvious draw-back—that the Army, because traditionally it focused more upon men as individuals than on weapons systems, was relatively poorly equipped in science. The Navy and Air Force had built up the power-ful research support needed for complex weapons systems like the through-deck cruisers and Harrier aircraft.

But Macfarlane's plan was not simply to give the Army a bigger share of the research budget. It aimed to create an organisation with fewer but bigger research units, yet one far more responsive to the fast-changing demands of defence. It regrouped the research centres into three broad technological functions that cut right across the three service arms. One of these functions is the basic technology—rocket motors, electronics, sensors, explosives—that could relate to a weapon for any arm of defence. The Royal Radar Establishment at Malvern, for instance, is now recognised as the focal point of all research on electronics and sensors—radar, night vision, laser guid-ance for bombs, etc.—for weapons systems.

Another group of research centres are now defined as the big-system centres. These will take the various pieces of technology of the first group and weave them into complex fighting systems—war-ships, aircraft, tanks, guided missiles. For the Air Force (the Royal Aircraft Establishment at Farnborough) and the Army (Fort Halstead in Kent), these big-system centres were easily chosen. For the Navy, which works in two quite different media—above and below water—the problem was harder, and was finally resolved by leaving the Navy with two big-systems centres, the Admiralty Surface Weapons Establishment near Portsmouth and the Admiralty Underwater Weapons Establishment near Weymouth.

One argument for fewer, bigger defence research centres is the saving in support costs. To take a single example, round-the-clock security at a multiplicity of small establishments is a heavy annual bill. Official figures for the savings from the closure of three research centres were an annual saving of £1·5 million on support services (not professional staff), for an initial outlay of £3 million.

But the bigger question is whether the Macfarlane plan has in-creased the efficiency of defence research projects by ensuring their completion on time and to the estimated cost. Will it prevent situa-tions like the Mark 24 torpedo, where the Navy scientists in the late 1960s failed to appreciate the complexity of the system required, and neglected to use the systems experience of guided missile develop-ment already available in Britain?

Some powerful safeguards were built into the plan. One was the role of the chief scientific adviser to the Secretary of State for Defence. Hermann Bondi, the ebullient cosmologist from King's College, has executive responsibility for the only one small laboratory, a 'think tank' for military strategy at Weybridge. But he has an overview of the entire research programme, and as chairman of the Defence Research Committee has direct control of the £51m. allocated 1974–5 for 'untargeted' research. Bondi's committee reviews all projects whose development costs exceed £2 million. It also reviews any project for which total production orders exceed £5 million; and any project that raises tricky political probems, such as those of special significance to industry.

Serving on this Defence Research Committee are Sir George Macfarlane's three deputies, each responsible for one of the broad technological functions of the research centres. But two of them also wear another hat. Quite independently of their responsibilities to Macfarlane they are also scientific advisers to one of the service arms. These are the fellows, they say, who oil the wheels of this vast research machine.

Customer–contractor relations

Thus the customer–contractor relationship in defence research is very clearly defined. The project directors in Whitehall are the 'customers'. Macfarlane's research centres are the 'contractors', who have to make sure they do not take on commitments they cannot fulfil. Bondi and his committee are a review body—and a referee to whom both parties can appeal.

Are these safeguards enough? Defence research, the mandarins admit, is part of a ponderous machine, as any of its size and complexity must be. They cannot guarantee that projects in future will not go awry in time and cost. No one can forecast precisely how many new aero-engines will have to be built and tested, how many missiles fired, before they will have an operational weapon. Quite minor aberrations can greatly increase research costs. They recall the guided missile which, because a safety feature (its destruct device) was less reliable than they wished, had to be transferred from Britain to Australia for its trials, at a huge increase in time and cost.

Transfer of the project from development—where it has been nursed affectionately by the people who spawned it—to production has also proved quite a hiccup for costs in the past. This is a problem that inevitably worsens with complexity in a system. Their answer here is to get the production people involved early in the research and development stage. In managing the business of defence research government scientists believe they have come a long way from the notorious TSR.2 project of the early 1960s, costing £1 million a week in research and development—with no end to the spending in sight.

CHAPTER 6

Can technology be controlled?

'If a decision is made not to make a decision, that is just as much a decision as a decision which initiates action.'

Adam Smith, *The Money Game*

Around the mid-1960s scientists at the (then) Ministry of Aviation began to chart in an ingenious new way the research costs of the TSR.2, a replacement for the Canberra bomber, by then costing about £4 million a month. What they learned was highly disturbing. The new 'cost slip' chart seemed to show that, after six years of research and development effort on TSR.2, there was still no end in sight to the escalating costs of this project. What in fact was happening was that the Service chiefs were trying, bit by bit, to turn a project for a Canberra replacement into a fully-fledged supersonic bomber—a project the government had killed years before.

Early in the 1970s Dr. Ieuan Maddock and his colleagues at the Department of Trade and Industry used the same technique to chart the costs of two civil projects whose research costs were becoming very worrisome: Concorde and the hovertrain. The shape of their charts followed closely the pattern of TSR.2 until it was axed in 1965. The hovertrain project was abandoned early in 1973. It had cost a total of £5 million—2·5 times the original estimate for demonstrating the feasibility of such a transport system. And it was poised to leap into a far more costly phase, with no trace of a possible customer in sight.

As with TSR.2, the decision to stop the hovertrain project brought forth a torrent of public protest from those financially or emotionally attached to the project. The protesters even included a Parliamentary Select Committee which, with several years' experience of scrutinising technical projects in Britain, might reasonably have been expected to take a more detached view.[1] As I wrote when it published its report vehemently criticising the government's decision, this committee might have written a very different report had it spent less time listening to the grievances of a handful of scientists

[1] *Tracked Hovercraft Ltd.*, Third Report from the Select Committee on Science and Technology, HMSO, 1973.

and engineers and paid more heed to the larger socio-economic questions involved. 'As it is, it has fallen right into the trap of supporting the view that technology should dictate the pace.'[1]

First Labour then Tory governments in Britain struggled hard to get off that particular hook. It was a line of thinking that led to a host of spectacular ventures—Concorde, hovercraft, vertical take-off airliners, sea-bed tractors, novel electricity generating systems—of highly dubious commercial value. The adventurous engineer's instincts, as I have said before, are always to see how far the technology will stretch.

The hovertrain project

Tracked Hovercraft was such a venture. Soon after the first hovercraft was unveiled in 1959, enthusiasts began to discuss a tracked version that might break right away from the 'steel-wheel-on-rail' systems. Speeds of several hundred m.p.h. were contemplated of hovertrains free from such restraints as adhesion and a rigid suspension. The original research on the hovertrain was done within a wholly-owned subsidiary of the National Research Development Corporation, called Hovercraft Development, but by the mid-1960s the research team was eager to launch a project on a scale large enough to demonstrate its claims. After some heart-searching, chiefly because no commercial interest showed the slightest sign of investing, the Labour government gave its approval in September 1967. A new wholly-owned NRDC subsidiary was formed, with Mr. Tom Fellows as chief executive and initial funds of £2 million.

Fellowes' brief was to explore on a large scale two inventions in which NRDC had proprietorial interest. One was Christopher Cockerell's air cushion suspension and the other was university research by Professor Eric Laithwaite of Imperial College, London, into linear induction methods of propulsion. A test track 3 miles in length was planned at a site near Cambridge, capable of extending to a twenty-mile track. Two further allocations of funds were approved by the government—albeit very reluctantly the second time—bringing the total to £5·25 million. For this sum the research team succeeded in running an unmanned test vehicle at speeds up to 107m.p.h., and thus demonstrating that the skills were there to take the project much further.

By 1971, however, a new government was asking much tougher questions than before. Here was a project all set to leap into the tens of millions of pounds bracket yet arousing no more enthusiasm

[1] David Fishlock, 'Why the hovertrain had to go', the *Financial Times*, 7 September 1973.

from potential backers at home or abroad than had been the case four years before. Other nations were showing great interest in the project—as was to be expected since they were pursuing similar projects—but none wished to join forces with Tracked Hovercraft. At no time during the life of the project—which included a spell of considerable publicity as it neared the end—did anyone offer to contribute significant sums to the work.

One important distinction between the hovertrain project and similar projects overseas was that all the others, although heavily government-supported, also involved private funds. For example, the three West German organisations in the field, Krauss-Maffei, Messerschmitt-Bolkow-Blohm and a consortium composed of Siemens, Brown Boveri and AEG, between them had chipped in about one-third of the £10 million or so spent by 1973 on such projects, with the government finding the rest. Locomotive makers in Britain such as Brush (Hawker Siddeley) and GEC showed no such enthusiasm to invest their own funds. One reason—the main one perhaps— was that British Rail showed no glimmer of interest in the hovertrain project for it could make no use of existing BR track. Past experience has taught British industry that untried systems which have found no market at home rarely find one abroad.

Another important distinction between the hovertrain and its rivals overseas was the inflexibility of the project. It was a project for a very high speed train, suitable only for long straight stretches of track, which would not adapt to the sinuous situations of urban transport requirements. Mr. Dennis Lyons, director-general of research at the Department of Environment, told the select committee bluntly that Tracked Hovercraft was 'on too fixed a direction and directed to too definite a project'. It was a view from the main potential customer for such a project that the select committee chose to ignore completely.

The APT project

Mr. Lyons's department is the one responsible for British Rail. In the mid-1960s British Rail had embarked on its own very ambitious project to develop a new and much faster train—yet one that would work with the existing track and signalling system. Track and signalling represent a capital investment of about £459 million (1972), an investment no one would abandon lightly. By exploring the limitations of the existing systems at a more fundamental level than ever before, British Rail's scientists at Derby produced a train concept tailored to the twists and bends of the track. For £5 million —the same sum as Tracked Hovercraft spent in developing a robot and one mile of new track—they had developed an experimental advanced passenger train (APT) replete with electronic controls and capable of running at 150m.p.h. on existing routes. What is more, they believed that the new principles on which it was based could be stretched to greater speeds, perhaps 200 or 250m.p.h. Such speeds might require some of the propulsion technology that was being developed for Tracked Hovercraft. But this possibility was scarcely justification—as the Select Committee seemed to be arguing—for also pursuing the alternative hovertrain project.

In a highly dubious attempt to justify their own project the hovertrain enthusiasts tried hard to cast doubt on the APT concept. The report quoted the 'distinguished academic witness' (unidentified) who assured the committee that at 150m.p.h. British Rail would be 'banging their heads against a limit'. The report argued that the government would be unwise to commit its future transport policy to a vehicle that had still to complete a technical proving programme. Yet that conclusion was reached at a time when the hovertrain was in so primitive a stage of development that not a single passenger had been able to travel upon it. The Germans, French, American and Japanese engineers who were pursuing very high-speed surface transport projects had all taken care to design test vehicles that could at least offer their patrons an exhilarating ride. Neither had British Rail, with its unique APT approach, neglected this important psychological point.

The Select Committee reached the conclusion that the government's decision to close down the hovertrain project was 'both premature and unwise'. Its case rested mainly on the fact that several other nations continued to put a major effort into high-speed surface transport.[1] Let us for the moment put to one side the argument— dubious though it is—that Britain should pursue a direction of research not because it is needed but because it is fashionable. Let us concentrate instead on one nation, West Germany, of similar size and ambitions to Britain, which is pursuing no less than three similar projects.

The German scene is worth studying more closely than the Select Committee—which took no evidence from the overseas projects— had bothered to do. First, government officials have told me frankly that they are very interested in British Rail's APT. This makes good sense, for Germany has a very highly developed system of existing railways, and plans to spend DM11,000 million (nearly £2,000 million) on their development by 1985, yet has no comparable pro-

[1] I once asked a group of West German Science Ministry officials in Bonn what 'magic formula' they used to pick the projects to back. The most senior man present said it was to look at what other countries like Britain were backing.

ject for extending performance. Second, the German programme which began in 1968—after Tracked Hovercraft was formed—rapidly became convinced that one of the two innovations Britain was trying to exploit was a non-starter. The much-vaunted air-cushion suspension was—to quote Krauss-Maffei, which claims to have built a test vehicle of this type more advanced than either Britain or France[1]—too noisy and too unstable. All three German projects have opted for magnetic levitation ('maglev') of various kinds. No more German money was to be spent on the air cushion.

Tracked Hovercraft's interest in 'maglev' had been confined to making paper studies once it became clear that the US, Japan and West Germany were all moving this way. Only after the axe fell in 1973 was any serious interest asserted in Eric Laithwaite's latest schemes for dual-purpose propulsion and levitation systems, using his so-called 'river of magnetism'. Bonn science officials had another point of importance to make: that they were supporting three industrial 'maglev' projects in the expectation that soon they would be able to choose the one of greatest promise and discontinue support for the other two.

One might wish it had come from a more dispassionate source, but Richard Marsh, chairman of British Rail, made a very pertinent comment to the Select Committee when he said it was 'one of the unique occasions when the Government has cancelled a project before it had wasted a great deal of public money'. Regrettably this remark probably accounts in part for the peevish tone of the report and the subtle efforts it makes to discredit British Rail's APT project —ironically on grounds that seem to argue simultaneously that it is too ambitious and not ambitious enough.

The 'eureka' factor

How on earth is the businessman, the civil servant, the Parliamentary Select Committee, to evaluate the advice—particularly the estimates of cost—he is given by scientists or engineers? To say: 'Pick a research manager you can trust' is no answer. How does a research manager evaluate the cries of 'eureka' from his own staff?

In chapter 3 we discussed the persistent tendency of the aviation industry to underestimate development costs by a factor of three or more. In chapter 5 we saw how difficult the Science Research Council had found it to pass judgment on the highly conflicting assertions of scientists in the field of robotics. Dr. Walter Marshall, member for research of the UK Atomic Energy Authority, told scientists at a National Academy of Sciences meeting in Washington in

[1] The French Aerotrain (hovertrain) project was abandoned in July 1974.

1973 that for any new programme 'the most important factor governing success is the sustained application of intelligence'.

What would or would not sell in the market place, what would or would not make a good business product, could all be decided by the careful application of logical thought, said Marshall. But it was logical thought 'somewhat different', he warned, from scientific thought processes, with a discipline of its own.

If any one person can be held responsible for steering the Select Committee and, by his television appearances, a great many members of the general public, to a false conclusion about the hovertrain it is probably Professor Eric Laithwaite. Science has comparatively few really colourful fellows of high academic repute and the capacity to grip a lay audience with excitement at the ideas they propound. Laithwaite is certainly one of the few. A big, boisterous fellow with a broad north country accent and a penchant for the right biblical quotation, he takes great delight in surprising or astonishing an audience.

No modest man, Laithwaite lets it be known that he is the world's greatest authority on a type of electrical propulsion, little used yet but likely to find large markets in the future, known as the linear induction motor (LIM). Where most engines are designed to drive a shaft round and round, the LIM—like the jet engine—propels in a straight line. In Laithwaite's adroit hands it can be made to eject a shell from a cannon or to simultaneously levitate and propel a model train long a track. His audience is treated to an exhilarating verbal and visual display in which objectivity towards either his own ideas and inventions or those of his rivals plays a secondary part.

Of his own work on the LIM, Laithwaite has been claiming—he was even quoted in the scientific Press as claiming—'we're six years ahead of everybody and we intend to stay there'.[1] Such a claim is probably unwarranted for *any* new idea or invention of recognisable commercial or military value today.

However, in a more reflective moment during the month his claim was published, Laithwaite admitted to me that the hovertrain project, to which he was consultant, promised him opportunities to try out his latest ideas for large-scale linear motor systems that he could not afford to explore in his laboratory at Imperial College, London, and which (as a part-time businessman himself) he would not expect either GEC or Linear Motors, the companies with which he is associated, to finance themselves. With disarming frankness he admitted that between the four centres of interest in linear motors 'we had it made'—until the government wielded its axe. Nevertheless, he stood by his claim of a six-year lead.

[1] *Physics Bulletin*, September 1973.

Some research managers claim to know their man well enough to be able to apply a factor—it might be called the 'optimism factor' or the 'eureka factor'—to each individual in a position to put forth substantial requests for funds. This is the factor by which the boss mentally multiplies the sum requested before deciding whether to fund the project. For one man the 'eureka factor' might be say 1·2, for another it might be two, three or some still greater figure.

But what on earth should one make of such projects as the Sydney Opera House, an adventurous piece of engineering in concrete but scarcely to be classed as high technology? The estimated cost of £3 million in 1958 rose to £40 million before its completion in 1973— a factor of thirteen. More adventurous engineering was the deep-sea rescue programme of the us Navy, where an initial proposal to build twelve rescue craft for $36·5 million escalated to $480 million for six craft only—a factor of twenty-seven.

Had the politicians and civil servants concerned with aerospace projects in Britain since the war had their 'eureka factor' to apply to proposals, Britain might have indulged in fewer costly failures. A retrospective appraisal has shown that British aerospace projects since the Second World War pretty consistently underestimated their costs by a factor of more than three. Mr. R. Nicholson, programme director of Rolls-Royce's RB.211 aero-engine project at the time of the crash, when asked by the government's inspectors what went wrong with his project, admitted that he couldn't improve on the statement: 'We failed to appreciate it was going to cost us so much.' Confessed Nicholson to his inquisitors: 'We ought to have known, there is no question. We just have to look at the history of projects through the 1960s.'[1] The £65 million project estimate in 1968 finally turned out to be a bill for £195 million—a factor of three.

The factor of about three had, in fact, been suggested some years before. In a lecture on 'The development of inventions' in 1970 T. A. Coombs remarked that the ratio of actual time and cost to estimated time and cost of development programmes was not two, as had been believed during the 1950s, but π.[2] But even when experience had shown what could happen, he said, people maintained an outrageous optimism. 'I was recently told, with a use of words which would have delighted Sir Ernest Gowers, "We do not anticipate any difficulties." The unfortunate thing is that almost everything unexpected that happens to a development project is bad.' From this Mr. Coombs concluded, however, that 'it is therefore

[1] *Rolls-Royce Limited*, Department of Trade and Industry Report by R. A. MacCrindle QC and P. Godfrey FCA., HMSO, 1973.
[2] T. A. Coombs, Institution of Mechanical Engineers, 11 November 1970.

just as well that one does not know too much otherwise one would never start anything new'.

Most persistent defect

The reluctance of the engineer to take costs into account was possibly his most persistent defect, Dr. Ieuan Maddock, chief scientist at the Department of Industry, told engineers gathered in London in October 1973 during his presidential address to the Institution of Electronic and Radio Engineers. He found this reluctance to face the full significance of costs in nearly every project—

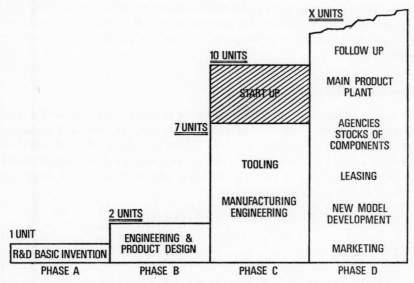

Figure 7 Four phases in the innovation process—each more expensive than its predecessor.

'a fair number by now'—with which he had come in contact. He confessed, moreover, that he himself had been guilty of the same defect when advancing projects of his own in the past.[1]

Maddock isolated a number of reasons why very few projects in advanced technology stayed within their cost forecasts. One was that the man with the idea failed to appreciate that for each unit spent on research and development, the project would require ten units to bring it to the market place—and might need as many as a hundred units to fully exploit a market (*see figure 7*). This fourth phase of ex-

[1] David Fishlock, 'How to read the warning signals', the *Financial Times*, 6 November 1973.

ploitation included expanded or modernised production plant, stockpiling of parts, creation of agencies, provision of leasing finance and extended credit—all factors that tended to be completely forgotten in the early stages of a project. Another reason for escalating costs was that the difficulties bound to arise as projects are expanded from the conceptual to the practical scale are consistently underestimated. The error is particularly great when disciplines outside the person's own knowledge and experience are required, as is increasingly the case with high technology projects today. These other disciplines the engineer tended to dismiss as 'mere engineering detail', said Maddock. A third reason for escalating costs was deliberate underestimating by the engineer, who even argued sometimes that if their estimate were to include realistic margins for contingency the project would never be approved at all. Such an argument ignores the annoyance subsequent revelations are likely to cause the sponsor.

The cost-slip chart

In the cost-slip chart the Department of Industry has a powerful way of diagnosing the disease of cost escalation. It was a technique borrowed from the Ministry of Aviation, where they devised a method to try to keep track of big defence projects whose costs showed a tendency to run amok. They plot a chart, the horizontal axis of which is the ratio:

$$\frac{\text{Current estimate of remaining cost}}{\text{Original estimate of total cost}}$$

and the vertical axis of which is the ratio:

$$\frac{\text{Money spent so far}}{\text{Original estimate of total cost}}$$

(The effects of inflation are removed, of course, in order to present the curve at constant prices.)

Cost escalation can be very dramatically exposed by the cost-slip chart. The project whose costs are under control yields a sloping line at 45 degrees from unity on one axis to unity on the other. *Figure 8* shows the curve for Concorde—which 'walks up the page'. As the project progressed cost estimates were revised at intervals, giving a line that zig-zags its way vertically up the chart. As the reader will see, this cost-slip curve stands at present a little further from its target than when the project began back in 1962. Maddock described the Concorde project as 'one of the most publicised and best documented

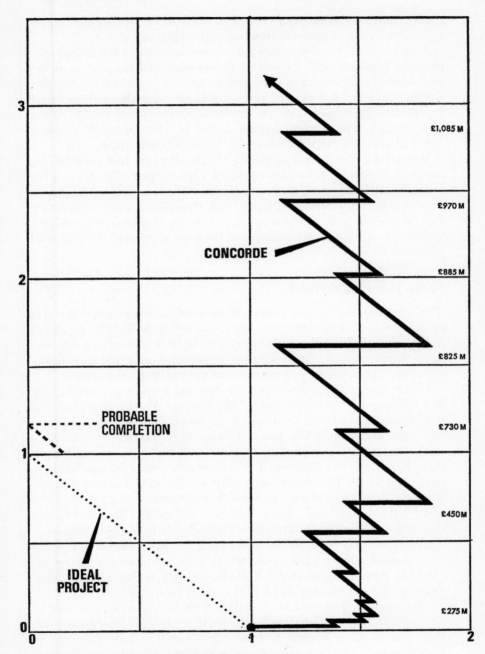

Figure 8 Cost-slip curve for the Concorde project.

cases of cost escalation', not because it was special but because it was typical of so many projects in advanced technologies.

Figure 9 gives cost-slip curves for two other British high technology projects, however—the prototype fast reactor at Dounreay and the steam-generating heavy water reactor (SGHWR) at Winfrith. Despite the fact that the fast reactor project was running about three years behind its original schedule, the curve conforms closely to that of the idea project. The SGHWR, commissioned in 1969, actually yields a curve that meets the vertical axis at a point below unity.

But Maddock told his audience bluntly that he had seen all too many and diverse examples of projects whose cost-slip charts were 'walking up the page', like Concorde's. Once a project began to display this characteristic the time had arrived to examine its future with a critical eye. 'This may well call for courageous decisions, which are certain to be unpopular in some quarters,' he observed with wry irony.

Projects under control

The cost-slip curve can reveal dramatically when the time has arrived to abandon a project. What it cannot do is keep a project under control. That the costs of projects in high technology can and do sometimes remain under control is perhaps best stated by offering a few examples, together with some of the reasons advanced.

Of four private unaided ventures into the aero-engine market by Rolls-Royce between the end of the Second World War and the RB.211 project in 1968, three failed to pay off. The Tyne engine was not a financial success; the Medway and Trent projects were cancelled by the prospective customers. But the Spey engine, although initially a strain on the company's finances, was making profits by 1970. Developed originally for the civil airliner market, it eventually powered no less than five aircraft: two civil (Trident and BAC 1–11) and three military (Nimrod, Buccaneer and Phantom). The official inquiry on Rolls-Royce found that engineering costs actually incurred in developing the Spey family of engines were commendably close to forecast. This achievement above all seems to have convinced the Rolls-Royce Board that its engineers' estimates for developing the RB.211 could be trusted.

The Spey project was launched in 1962 at an estimated cost of £30 million—approximately the figure it finally cost. So pleased was Rolls-Royce that it even sent teams around Britain and the US boasting that it knew how to cost precisely a project in high technology. In fact the government's inspectors commented that the precision of the estimate was 'not wholly surprising' when one considered

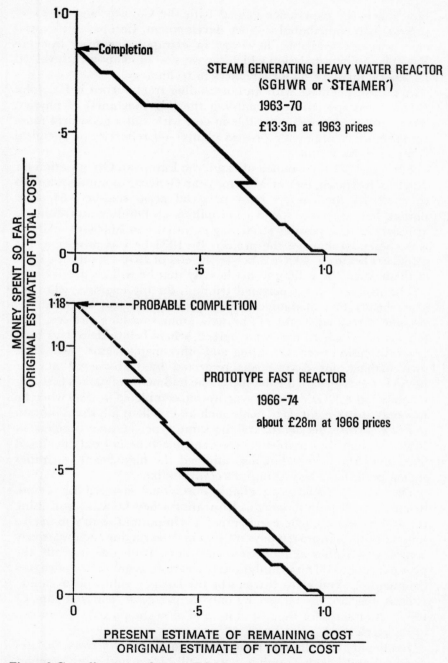

Figure 9 Cost-slip curves for two British prototype nuclear reactors.

how much the experience gained with the Conway and Medway projects had contributed to Spey development. Comparable experience was not available, however, in extrapolating from Spey to RB.211—an extrapolation which, as we saw in chapter 3, involved no less than twelve major advances in technology.

A project engineer with an outstanding track record is Dr. John Adams who specialises in building the 'big machines' of physics. These are machines comparable in cost with and a good deal more complex than large-scale process plants—oil refineries or chemical complexes, for instance.

Early in 1971 the Council of CERN, the European Organisation for Nuclear Research, met at Meyrin, near Geneva, to approve a plan to construct the world's most powerful atom smasher. Member nations had agreed to spend £114 million on building a machine of at least 200GeV, possibly stretching eventually to 1,000GeV. Adams was chosen to manage the project. By 1973 he was promising the physicists beams of 400GeV before the end of 1976—a promise most of them would be willing to bet heavily that he will keep.

The decision was a personal triumph for the engineer who two years before had abandoned a top government post in Britain to become director-general of the new atom smashing project. The scheme on which all now were agreed, where before there had been great dissension over cost, siting and other major factors, was of his own making, for Adams was respected by high-energy nuclear physicists everywhere for the success he had made of CERN's first 'big machine', the 28GeV proton synchroton, completed in 1959 when he was only thirty-eight. (He made such an excellent job that Nimrod, a 7GeV British accelerator of the same type, became obsolescent before it could be completed; the CERN machine not only achieved four times the energy but also attained the high beam intensities that were to have been Nimrod's contribution.)

Dr. Adams displays an almost obsessional concern for detail. Scientists in Britain found this frustrating when he was scrutinising research proposals, where sometimes it is important simply to back a hunch. But his approach pays off well in constructing such massively complex machines as modern accelerators. Each one is really the prototype for a still more ambitious project; so, as one of his colleagues commented, 'You know it won't be the last you will want to build.' Adams overshot his budget by only 20 per cent—a trivial sum by today's standards for the first of its kind of so complex an instrument as an accelerator.

His deputy and disciple then, Dr. Kjell Johnsen of Norway, later designed and is now running CERN's still bigger and more complex intersecting storage rings. This research tool takes the beam of protons from the 28GeV accelerator, splits it and sends the two parts whirling in opposite directions round tunnels 330 yards in diameter. Then the two beams are steered into head-on collision, liberating more of what the physicists call 'creative energy' than any other machine existing today. Johnsen completed the construction task in 1970, within the budget (£37 million) and time-scale approved five years before.

'It's no miracle,' says Johnsen, 'we've consciously tried very hard to stay within our targets.' Too often, he says, those engaged in advancing technology tend to overlook the cost of engineering details when extrapolating from previous projects, so up goes the cost. 'And of course if you are late it will cost more too.' This attention to detail was sometimes sadly lacking in the design of commercial nuclear plants, with the results described in chapter 4.

Nuclear plant, as we have seen, is a complex integration of novel materials and technologies, representing far deeper and quicker excursions into the unknown than the most adventurous ideas in aviation. Whereas Britain completed the world's first sizeable nuclear plant, Calder Hall, in three and a half years, by the 1970s plants of five or six times its electrical capacity were taking up to ten years to complete. Even then many months might elapse before the plant achieved acceptably high levels of output and availability.

There were very few exceptions, such as the Tsuruga plant in Japan, completed in four and a half years. But the truly outstanding exception has been the Canadian Pickering station near Toronto, the world's biggest nuclear plant (2,000MW) at the time of writing, where not one but four reactors have been commissioned on time and performed in a manner remarkable by nuclear standards so far. Its first reactor, for instance, was available for electricity generation for 80 per cent of the time in its first year—an unprecedented performance for a new commercial reactor.

Pickering is based on Canada's own nuclear reactor design, the Candu reactor, developed and constructed by the state-owned company Atomic Energy of Canada Limited (AECL). Its president, J. Lorne Gray, an engineer of international standing in the nuclear business, firmly believes that the customer-contractor relationship his company has built with Pickering's owners is the foundation of the project's success.[1] The utility, Ontario Hydro—Canada's biggest —now has a 10,000MW nuclear programme based on the Candu reactor.

Ontario Hydro—whose Latin motto translates as 'the gifts of nature are for the people'—has traditionally designed and managed

[1] David Fishlock, 'Nuclear power—Canada's offer of help', the *Financial Times*, 14 June 1972.

construction of all its power stations. When nuclear power came along it joined forces with AECL to build Douglas Point, a 220MW prototype Candu reactor. 'We took a lot of stick over Douglas Point,' said one utility executive, 'but if your prototype works well you don't learn very much.' (Britain's prototype reactors, by the way, performed outstandingly well.) Many and vexing were the problems at Douglas, but the lessons were learned and fed into the design of commercial stations.

Pickering was ordered as a group of four identical units, a policy Ontario Hydro had evolved for its fossil fuel plants during the 1960s. It gave Canadian industry a chance to tool up for a run of components. Replication, as it is called, had two crucial effects for Ontario Hydro. First, it cut costs—costs at Pickering fell for each successive unit to come on-load. The other effect was that should something go awry, say on test, there was an excellent chance when components were ordered in sets of four of 'cannibalising' a later unit. When the 500MW turbo-generator for Pickering 2 caught fire on test, the unit for Pickering 3 was wheeled in to replace it. In the event, the faulty machine had to be returned to England and rewound, which would have meant a delay of twelve to eighteen months had the utility not had a replacement. It finally found its niche in Pickering 4.

Another factor Ontario Hydro believes is important to its success at Pickering is the extent to which the Candu design of reactor can be tested and 'debugged' before the reactor itself goes critical. The engineers can run all the systems on the nuclear side almost up to operating conditions while the station is still under construction. This shortens the time to run to full power, they say, from months to weeks or even to a few days.

One further factor in project management of which the utility is very proud is the way it integrates its design, construction and operations staff into a single team to commission the plant. 'We even put our designers out into the field.' The activities of this team are very critically phased into the final stages of construction of each unit, to minimise the delays.

These, then, are the techniques—simple enough in concept—that have enabled AECL and Ontario Hydro to bring Pickering into service faster than any other multi-reactor station anywhere in the world. 'The magic formula I keep quoting,' says Dr. John Foster, vice-president in charge of power projects for AECL, 'is experience.' This experience is now being applied to another four-unit nuclear station, the 3,000MW Bruce station on Lake Huron, for the same customer. Bruce is scheduled to produce its first power in 1976. The big question now is whether Britain, having chosen (July 1974) for its third nuclear programme a reactor (the SGHWR) very similar to

Canada's Candu reactor, will also adopt the techniques the Canadians credit with the undisputed success of their nuclear power programme.

Contract research and project control

The research contract is my final example of a proven technique for keeping control of high technology, at least in the early stages. It works both ways. It works when a research manager sub-contracts his requirements to a team in which he has confidence, on strict conditions of time-scale and price. Instead of committing his own staff and resources in the early stages he commits someone else's, leaving himself free to take a more dispassionate view of progress and prospects. It can also work when the research manager makes part of his own research capacity available for solving other people's problems, for this way he can get a valuable feedback about the competitiveness of his own research costs.

In theory, contract research caters for those who do not have research and development resources of their own. The customer buys his scientific advice just as he might use the specialised services of an architect, a surveyor or a consulting engineer. When special investigations are needed the contract research organisation quotes for the task, and advises its client on the chances of success.

In practice, contract research usually caters for those who already have extensive research facilities and a good appreciation of the problems and pitfalls of managing research and development. Except in the sector of scientific services—assay, evaluation, testing and special reports—the principal customers for contract research are government and the bigger, research-conscious companies. Sadly, those who most urgently need the services of contract research, to improve, update or completely replace obsolescent products and production techniques, are the ones least likely to hire them. Too often they fail to recognise that they have a problem at all.

The most glamorous success story of contract research concerns xerography, a brilliant one-man idea for document copying that broke right away from established principles of photography, into an 'opto-electronic' technology. In the three decades since its inventor made a deal with a contract research organisation, xerography has grown into a corporation with earnings in 1971 of about £800m. Xerox Corporation is one of the 'three senior sisters of growth' on Wall Street—all companies making this money from the management of high technology. (The others are IBM and Polaroid.)

As a patent attorney before the Second World War, Chester Carlson occasionally came into contact with the Battelle Memorial

D

Institute, a contract research organisation in Columbus, Ohio. In 1944, after trying for several years to interest manufacturers in his ideas, Carlson signed an agreement with the Battelle Development Corporation, commercial arm of the organisation. Battelle became his agent, free to develop his invention and grant licences under his us and Canadian patent. In return, Carlson was to receive 40 per cent of all royalties, and Battelle the other 60 per cent.[1]

Over the next two years the research organisation contributed two major advances to the original idea—a method of coating plates with the amorphous, photo-conductive form of selenium, and a corona discharge wire for transferring the electrostatic charge to this plate and for transferring powder from plate to paper. Carlson, impressed with this progress, raised enough cash to maintain his full equity in the royalties when the time came to inject more cash.

Commercial support came in 1946 from the Haloid Company, which made an agreement with Battelle to license the invention and which in return was to sponsor further research by Battelle for up to $25,000 a year. Both sides took a big gamble in making this deal: Haloid because its total profits that year had been only $101,000, and Battelle because it was backing a relatively small and financially weak organisation against the big battalions of the graphic arts industry. Between 1946 and 1960, when Haloid launched its 914 xerox automatic office copier, the company invested $40m in research and development. The following year it changed its name to Xerox Corporation. Battelle continued to work on research sponsored by Xerox and by 1970 had notched up no less than 164 patents in the invention. Battelle's share of the revenue amounted to almost 100 times its original $3·5m endowment. In 1973 Xerox Corporation —a company born of research—re-invested about $150 million of its earnings in the science of new copying technology, so great is its confidence that this is the way to maintain its growth.

[1] George A. W. Boehm and Alex Groner, *The Battelle Story: Science in the Service of Mankind*, D. C. Heath, 1972, pp. 35–49.

CHAPTER 7

Electronics: the art of control

'One of the great strategies of science and technology is to do the easiest things first. Well, we've been doing that for about 100 years now, and the problems have become much tougher.'

Dr. William O Baker, president of Bell Telephone Laboratories, quoted in *Forbes*, 1974

Sir Arnold Weinstock is chief executive of the General Electric Company, Britain's largest engineering company with sales exceeding £1,100 million a year and a product range that divides into two roughly equal groups. One might be called 'conventional' electrical products: motors, turbo-generators, switchgear, television sets, domestic appliances. The other is 'high technology': military and space electronics, telecommunications, computers, automation systems, nuclear steam supply systems.

Weinstock, a rather shy statistician with a cool calculating approach to commerce, brusquely dismisses any idea that the two types of product need different approaches by management. He admits, however, that high technology implies you have got to be clever to succeed at it—'which tends to keep people out'. He acknowledges, too, a pejorative use of the expression 'high technology', meaning high-risk business. 'But it is not high-risk—we know what we are doing.' In his view—one confirmed by experience gained through the acquisition in the late 1960s of two companies, English Electric and AEI, deep in trouble with high technology projects—managing high technology is mainly a matter of making sure that any given business operation has available the full range of managerial skills—including the technical skills—needed to meet the chosen market.[1]

By British industry standards Weinstock is spending generously on research. Including the money he received in research contracts from government departments, his research and development budget amounts to some £70 million a year.[2] It is large by British industry standards, comparable for example with the research budgets of ICI and Royal Dutch Shell. It is small, however, by the standards of some of Weinstock's rivals in the electronics sector: for instance, such

[1] 'GEC's future with cash in the bank', the *Financial Times*, 23 July 1973, p. 25.
[2] Nicholas Valéry, 'Biggest science budget in the business', *New Scientist*, 27 September 1973, p. 740.

giants as the Bell System, IBM and Philips. It is worth examining the motivation of these three companies for spending as much as a tenth of turnover on research and development, much of it at a level indistinguishable from the best academic research in the field; at a level, in fact, that has earned Nobel Prizes.

Electronics is not a clearly defined industrial sector, comparable say with the motor car or chemical process industries, but a very powerful technique for measurement and control. It is the technique of sensing and amplifying information, processing it and using it to control systems—industrial, weapon, communication, entertainment and many other kinds of system. Already electronics permeates almost all human activity, from warfare to welfare (with electronic care of the sick).

Yet the potential scope for electronics remains immense—for one simple reason. In contrast to most kinds of high technology (which must work very hard at, say, raising a temperature to make any progress), the cost of doing things by electronics has been falling at an astonishingly rapid rate. The key is microminiaturisation, a craft born of chemisty and physics, which in a decade or so has demonstrated conclusively that within a few years the cost of performing any given function of measurement or control is going to be infinitesimally small.

To this remarkable record of research achievement can be added the pull of an intellectual challenge of a different kind. The central problem in any electronic system is always to distinguish clearly and unambiguously the signal you want from the clutter of other signals. In a military context the situation is complicated immensely by deliberate efforts to distort or obliterate the relevant signal. Where military electronics are being studied, work on electronic countermeasures is always nearby, challenging the best brains available to defeat any new system. Some civil sectors, notably computers and telecommunications, also have their security problems, again engaging the best minds that can be hired.

Bell Laboratories

On a hillside a few miles south of New York stands a long building of salmon-pink brick where in 1947 a physicist scribbled a colleague a hasty invitation to 'a conference . . . to demonstrate some effects, 10.45 this am. Everything has been arranged at short notice. Since your group has contributed so much help to our job, I hope you can break away and come.' The recipient went. He knew the 'job' and how big an event could be disguised in the phrase 'some effects', for it involved a crystal he had painstakingly prepared and purified. It was the birth of the transistor, when a chip of crystal more perfect than gemstone was made to behave like a radio valve.

Few inventions can claim so profound an influence on society as the development of the transistor by Bell Telephone Laboratories at Murray Hill. In the early years of its life the device was rechristened the 'persistor' by one of the inventors—it took so much persistence to make it work at all. But by 1956, when William Shockley, John Bardeen and Walter Brattain shared the Nobel Prize for Physics, the 'transistor effect' had begun to transform the world of electronics.

Within a year or two the first integrated circuits were made; arrays of electronic components engraved within a single chip of crystal. The scientists had taken their first tentative steps on the path of microminiature electronics, a path along which the number of components possible in an integrated circuit doubled each year down through the 1960s, while costs per component tumbled 10,000-fold compared with the first transistors. Bell scientists confidently forecast progress of the same order through the 1970s.

It is probably true that had Bell not invented the transistor and set electronics upon this immensely productive path of micro-miniaturisation, someone else would have done so. It is also true to say that virtually no other laboratories, industrial or academic, in the 1940s and early 1950s had all three essential ingredients—the motivation, the talent and the resources—to solve such a formidable problem. For Bell the problem had been posed in the 1930s when its scientists recognised that as the Bell System, the world's largest telephone network, continued to grow in size and complexity the radio valve would present a huge limitation. It was too big, too fragile, too hungry for power. Hope for a replacement, Bell scientists saw, lay in the fledgling science of solid-state physics. War interrupted their plans but as soon as hostilities ceased, Shockley began to assemble a brilliant team that in little more than two years fashioned from a curiosity called germanium a new amplifier of electric current.

Perhaps two other laboratories in the entire world had the three essential ingredients to make the invention at about that time. Both have longer if not quite such lustrous records of contributions to science, for both laboratories date back to the turn of the century, whereas Bell Laboratories were born only in 1925. One is the research centre of us General Electric (no relation of the British company of that name) in Schenectady, New York. The other is Philips research centre in Eindhoven, Holland. Together with Bell Laboratories, these research centres freely interchange their scientists with universities in a way that is rare in other industrial laboratories. In the 1960s they were joined by a fourth, ibm, whose big new research centre at Yorktown Heights, New York, also undertook science at an academically highly respectable level. Scientists with the IBM and US General Electric laboratories shared the 1973 Nobel Prize for Physics with a British scientist at the University of Cambridge for contributions to solid-state physics.

By normal standards of industrial research all four laboratories have a quite remarkable degree of freedom in what they pursue and what resources they bring to bear on a problem, although they are not entirely free to go their own ways. Murray Hill for example, with 3,600 staff, is only part—roughly a quarter—of Bell Telephone Laboratories, probably the largest industrial research organisation anywhere in the world. Most of the rest of Bell's scientific effort goes into the development of telecommunications equipment and manufacturing technology for the Bell System. At Murray Hill the task is to try to colonise territories of science whose application to the Bell System is 'very uncertain—even very improbable—but not ridiculous', as one senior research worker puts it.

Nuclear (low-energy) physics was chosen as such a field; and so it turned out, with relevance to ion beam implantation, an up-and-coming method of making microminiature electronics. High-energy (atom smashing) physics was and still is considered 'ridiculous' in the Bell context.

To fulfil its task the Murray Hill scientists believe they must participate fully in the scientific community. But as many a research director has learned the hard way this is not so easily done. You can buy solutions to many problems if you know how and where to communicate with the world of science. What you cannot hope for is to get solutions to problems that do not yet exist, that you cannot yet formulate clearly; or to get ideas for using inventions or effects of which you yourself have never heard.

So the logic is clear. Only by participating in the world of scientific discovery and advance can an organisation expect to stay abreast of ideas that may find no commercial application for ten, twenty, perhaps thirty years. The entrance fee here is not cash or contracts or other kinds of patronage but contributions to progress— contributions that meet the exacting criteria of science itself. Such a commitment to scholarship demands infinite patience and a very long purse.

IBM Research Division

Dr. Lewis Branscomb, vice-president and chief scientist of IBM, responsible directly to the company's chief executive for the 'long-term overview' of a $670 million (1973) research and development

effort, describes his job as 'counteracting the overwhelming pressures
to sub-optimise for tomorrow'.

Worldwide, IBM has twenty-six major laboratories, but Branscomb
himself has no line responsibility. As he puts it, 'I'm the one person
in the company with no excuse for failing to see the trees.' His job
is to try to answer such questions as: 'Suppose logic and memory
were free, how would society use them and make them secure?'
IBM's laboratories, notably its $50 million-a-year research division,
are already well down the path of miniaturisation towards a logic
and memory that for all practical purposes will be free.

So that commercial pressures can never distract the company from
its long-range goals, IBM segregates its scientific effort in an autono-
mous research division under Ralph Gomory as director of research.
Like Branscomb, Dr. Gomory is also a vice-president, reporting
directly to the same chief. But, Gomory is quick to point out, the research division is no 'ivory tower'. For one thing, it has no less than three
research centres, several thousand miles apart: at Yorktown Heights
near New York, the headquarters, and also in Zürich and San José.

Another and more important reason is simply that Gomory's goals
are so ambitious that should they succeed, the product divisions
would have little hesitation about using the new technology. His
formula for success is to put present and future technologies into
direct competition at the research level. He has scientists trying to
stretch present computer technologies to new limits, working right
alongside scientists with ideas that could leapfrog those limits.

The 'bubble memory' is such an idea. Scientifically, the idea of
storing information as minute specks or 'bubbles' of magnetism, and
shunting them along tracks like trucks round a marshalling yard, is
tremendously exciting. The scientist can actually see what is happening under the microscope. Technologically it is still more startling,
for 'bubbles' could do for information storage—one of the clumsier
aspects of present-day computers—what the integrated circuit is
already doing for logic, by way of shrinking the volume, the power
required and the cost.

The idea of the bubble memory was born of university research in
Europe, and advanced through the research efforts of several companies, including Philips, Bell Laboratories and IBM. Several years of
intensive effort from the late 1960s brought the bubble memory to a
stage in 1972 where a microminiature computer could be built with
its help. But the expense and difficulty of harnessing bubbles still
seemed to outweigh any likely advantage—testimony to the remarkably sophisticated state of the electro-mechanical systems and the
development potential they still have.

Then, at a point when others were cutting back their research effort, IBM's research division announced that it had harnessed bubbles fifty times smaller than anyone else, in a new kind of material, much cheaper and easier to fabricate. The implications are immense: storage at densities tens of thousands of times greater than are known today, and manufacture by methods akin to those already used to make logic. Storage and logic, two of the three primary sectors of any computer, could then be brought together in one highly condensed component. IBM's announcement rekindled efforts worldwide to develop magnetic bubble storage systems for tomorrow's computers. With computing power now threatening to add appreciably to world energy needs—the 90,000 computers in the US today are already believed to draw 1·5 to 2 per cent of US energy needs—a super-dense, all-solid-state computer promises dramatic reductions in the electrical input.

But if bubbles fail to come off, Gomory has two other ideas, no less ambitious, for super-dense storage. One, like bubbles, came from academic research in Europe. The Josephson effect was predicted in Cambridge in 1962. Scientists in IBM's research division were quick to recognise the implications and began to develop a 'superconducting' memory cell capable of switching at speeds far beyond the electronic components used in computers today; speeds so great that light would travel only a few millimetres while the device was operating. As with bubbles, both logic and memory using the Josephson junction can be made by the same techniques.

The third idea of superdense storage was born within IBM's own research division. Here the idea is to design and make a wholly synthetic substance known as a 'super-lattice', so perfect in structure that electrons would be far better behaved than in any material used today. Dr. Leo Esaki, an eminent Japanese scientist who has already given his name to one semiconductor device, and who shared (with Dr. Brian Josephson of Cambridge) the 1973 Nobel Prize for physics, has recently begun to design and make super-lattices. Using a very high vacuum technique under the control of a computer, he deposits alternate layers of two different semiconductors, each layer only three to five atoms thick. These are early days yet for a novel and very difficult approach. But already Esaki has seen the first indications that his super-lattice will have the very powerful properties he predicts.

Electronic concepts as far advanced as these can emerge, says Gomory, only by giving outstandingly creative people their head. Such people—and they include Gomory himself, a mathematician of considerable acclaim—would work for IBM only if it created conditions conducive to the best science. 'Some of our work would be very hard to distinguish from that of the university professor.'

When to stop

But even organisations as large and prosperous as these electronic giants have limits to their patience and purse when the commitment is as open-ended as science. The plain facts are that the probability of a company using the results of any given piece of its research is pretty small. Using science well is much harder than getting it done, points out Branscomb, adding that most technologists are just not sensitive enough to the 'fine tuning of customer needs'.

Decisions—sometimes very harsh decisions—have still to be taken if the research programme is to remain coupled to the company's own commercial aspirations. Late in 1972 Bell Laboratories took such a decision in cutting right back on its work on the holographic memory, an exciting concept scientifically but one which it reckoned would demand too big a research investment to harness to telephone technology.

A problem of fine-tuning which Bell's scientists failed to anticipate cost the organisation at least \$100 million. This is the cost—very difficult to define precisely, so widely was the research effort spread— of developing a video telephone system called Picturephone.[1] Although, technically speaking, Picturephone was an astonishingly successful research and development project, the system today is virtually in cold storage. Thirty years of research work on video telephony by Bell, begun before the Second World War, had failed to prepare the company for the entirely new kind of man–machine relationship it was attempting to market.

The Bell System first announced Picturephone in the mid-'sixties. They were beginning to build a market image that one Bell executive has described as 'grandma talking to the kids'. By the mid-1970s the organisation expected many thousands of homes in the US to have a telephone service that allowed grandma not merely to hear but to see her grandchildren at distances of hundreds and thousands of miles. Incredibly, Picturephone needed only three pairs of normal telephone wires to carry both audio and video signals.

The original market dream began to crumble when New York vetoed the company's plans to mount a big sales campaign in that city. The city fathers said bluntly that Bell had to put POTS—the plain old telephone service—right first. An unforeseen growth in demand, especially for the stock market, had coincided with the introduction of electronic telephone switching and the result was a chaotic deterioration in the telephone service around the late 1960s.

Meanwhile, the man–machine problem had begun to loom large. This was not just a question of the unacceptability of a black-and-

[1] *Science and Government Report*, vol. 3, no. 16, 1973.

white portrait in a country that had seen its scientists televising the moon's surface in colour. People reacted unpredictably when faced with a television camera. There was the executive who, when linked by Picturephone to the desks of his directors, became so self-conscious about his bald head that he took to putting a hat on whenever anyone called him up. The camera automatically takes its cue for brightness from some highlight in the image it is transmitting and in this man's case it was using his shiny pate—with devastating results! Few were going to pay the telephone tariff Bell was asking for the opportunity to be embarrassed. For Bell's Holmdel Laboratories it was a case of 'back to the drawing board', to design systems specifically tailored to professional markets. For the present at least the domestic market is being quietly forgotten.

Philips' research

Academic acclaim since early this century has not deterred Philips, the Dutch electrical group, from asking sharp questions lately about the size and direction of its research effort. For as long as most of its scientists can remember the company has allocated some 7 per cent of turnover to research and development, about one quarter of which is spent on research. In 1972 the research sector alone, the company activity furthest removed from the market place, engaged the efforts of some 4,000 people and cost the company about £40 million—twice the budget of IBM's research division.

Directing Philips' central research effort since the retirement of the eminent Dutch physicist, Professor H. G. B. Casimir, in 1972, has been Dr. G. W. Rathenau who simultaneously shouldered the task of trying to make research more responsive to the people who pay the bill. This means the managers of Philips' fourteen product divisions —the company's entrepreneurs as the Board of Management sees them—who pay for central research through a levy on sales. Not only has research, a labour-intensive activity, been growing in cost through inflation, but it has also been demanding more and more research effort to make progress in the physical sciences. Rathenau's task, as he sees it, is to ensure that his clients remain satisfied in terms of new products and manufacturing techniques.

By the standards set by almost all other companies, Philips' research has kept quite remarkably free from what Lewis Branscomb would call 'pressures to sub-optimise for tomorrow'. Its scientists can expect more generous salaries and support than they would from a Dutch university, and the company has a high tolerance level to esoteric ideas on the off-chance that they may pay off. Even so, Philips' scientists have never been 'free'. The company wants the data they get. They are certainly not free to pursue research irrelevant to the company's commercial needs. Company research must behave 'like a well-trained gundog—but not a sheepdog', is how one senior Philips scientist puts it.

In reorganising Philips' research to try to make it more responsive to the future needs of the product divisions, Rathenau has tackled what he acknowledges to be the easiest part of the task. A childhood experience, when his father gave one doctor responsibility for his care in a life-and-death situation, taught him the value of giving one man full responsibility for a task. His research empire is spread over six laboratories in five countries, with roughly half in Eindhoven and the rest in Britain (the Mullard laboratories in Surrey), Hamburg, Aachen, Paris and Brussels. Each research centre now has responsibility for whole sectors of research—Hamburg for all company research on x-rays, for instance—and is instructed to make full use of the expertise of the other laboratories.

The harder part of Rathenau's task is to try to increase the productivity of the research laboratories by finding niches in the product divisions for an increasing proportion of their research data. It needs a fairly subtle approach for he recognises the risks of putting pressure on creative staff—'they could simply dry up', he says. 'Research lives on surprises. The most important thing for a research manager to do is to make sure the surprises are wanted.'

Philips has what it calls a 'push–pull philosophy' of research management, believing that successful innovation depends partly on the scientists pushing ideas at the product divisions, and partly on product divisions pulling innovations out of laboratories.[1] The balance between 'push' and 'pull' varies from division to division—the 'pull' element being strongest, of course, in products and techniques to which research has most to contribute. But the system works only when *both* forces are operating, emphasises Rathenau. As he sees it, his mission must be to increase the power of the 'pull' element. The efforts of one man especially, has helped to convince him that the research scientist in industry is wasting his time if he is doing something that sparks no response from the product divisions. 'You need the feedback from the division to get it just right.'

The man who brought this home to top management is Ir. M. van Tol, a scientist with ten years' experience in the research laboratories before moving to a product division. Today he is deputy manager of a product division that makes and markets a miscellany of research-based industrial equipment, from cyclotrons and many other research instruments to equipment and systems for welding, process control

[1] David Fishlock, 'How Philips' research swung from push to pull', the *Financial Times*, 27 June 1973.

and pollution monitoring. 'We pay towards research but have no say in how the money is spent—we can advise but not command', says Ir. van Tol. He likens research that lacks the interest and encouragement of a product division to an electrical circuit without a load. Everything may be in perfect working order but nothing flows.

His own failures as a research scientist to get ideas across to the product divisions led him to study the process of technology transfer. He soon convinced himself he was not alone; that a great deal of good Philips research never produced any profits. There were many reasons but the crucial one—and one he admits he had failed completely to spot while a researcher himself—was the inability of the famous Philips world-wide sales organisation to respond to many high-technology, industry-orientated innovations. Philips' salesmen knew little or nothing about the selling of professional equipment, yet this is the sector seen by the organisation as having the greatest potential for growth. Van Tol is also convinced that the trend for Philips' research must be to lay greater emphasis on the 'pull' element. 'We have to start asking about markets and whether the company has a sales organisation that could sell the equipment, before we start spending on research.' It means that key decisions have to be taken before a research proposal is ever approved. This in turn means that much more commercial information has to be assembled than is customary at this early stage in the innovative cycle.

Had Bell Laboratories adopted a 'push–pull' approach to Picturephone, the market place would have warned the company that, ingenious though its technology was, American homes were not ready to pay the price the Bell System was asking. In conversations late in 1972 at Bell's Holmdel Laboratories in New Jersey, where the Picturephone system was largely developed, I found the scientists had taken this expensive lesson to heart. They were still spending 'a few millions of dollars a year' on research, said Tom Powers, director of the telephone laboratory, but they were also deeply involved in the marketing aspects in trying to tailor Picturephone to the specific requirements of professional users, from telephone medical services to a real-estate service in which pictures, maps, floor plans could all be flashed on the client's screen. The 'tailoring' process extends as far back as research at Murray Hill on a new solid-state television camera and tube that could afford colour more cheaply than the previous black-and-white system, and as far forward as detailed marketing studies. 'We're learning a lot,' Powers admitted wryly.

In its vlp (video long-play) system, Philips' scientists have invented a piece of domestic electronics as revolutionary as Picturephone, which is expected to reach the market in the mid-1970s for about the same price as colour television. From a disc similar in size and appearance to an ordinary long-playing record can be recalled a colour picture and accompanying sound. The recording can be slowed, frozen, even reversed, at the touch of a button.

Like Picturephone, the VLP system is something people have talked of for many years, but the realisation of which had to wait for enough progress in several fields of science.[1] Could its market début prove as disastrous as that of Picturephone? One important reason why Philips is confident that its VLP system will receive a much more enthusiastic reception is the way it was born. It was 'pulled' from central research by a scheme put forward by one of its product divisions. A development engineer in Philips Electro-Acoustics Division had the idea of using a needle of laser light to read information from a spinning disc. He persuaded former colleagues in the research centre to try out the idea. Within three weeks they had a crude system that worked. By 1972 the division was ready to unveil the prototype of its new product and make its first declaration of intent to the market.

[1] *Philips Technical Review*, vol. 33, 1973, no. 7, pp. 178–93.

CHAPTER 8

Drugs: chemistry in harness

'. . . In an industry where the end product is virtually doomed to become obsolete in a few years, research is the very life blood.'

Sir Ronald Bodley-Scott, at the annual dinner of the Association of the British Pharmaceutical Industry, 1974

A significant yet still little recognised fact in the development of electronic technology is how far and how fast it is evolving from a piece-part industry dominated by engineers towards a process industry akin to the fine chemical and pharmaceutical industries. By about 1980 the chemists will be able to process individual chips of semiconductor to perform tasks equivalent to a million 'conventional' electronic components such as transistors and diodes. Thereafter the cost of logic and memory will plummet to vanishing point. 'Molecular engineering' of this kind will be but a step removed in scale from the chemistry of biologically active molecules, eagerly sought today by the pesticide, herbicide and pharmaceutical industries.

Like electronics, these industries are indisputably high technology. They demand a research expenditure not of the 1 or 2 per cent, customary in the engineering, metal and many other industries, but 8, 10, even 12 per cent of sales. Like electronics, they harness research skills at a level indistinguishable from academic research; but in the life sciences as well as the physical sciences. Unlike electronics, this top research talent is not necessarily confined to the discovery of new compounds and novel effects, but may well be harnessed at later stages in the protracted cycle from discovery to market (illustrated in *figure 10*). The most profound science in the evolution of a drug may not be the original discovery at all. It may well lie in discovering a method of synthesis for a complex compound that can be put safely and economically into production; it may lie in eliminating some undesirable side effect in the initial discovery, or even in finding a new way of administering a compound to the patient in order to bypass some body chemistry that would reduce its efficiency.

The point is made well by the story of the Beecham Group's rapid rise to become one of the top four pharmaceutical manu-

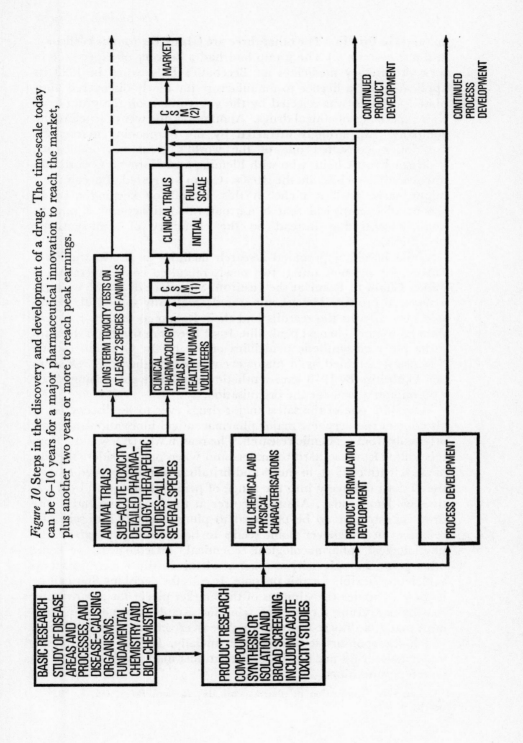

Figure 10 Steps in the discovery and development of a drug. The time-scale today can be 6–10 years for a major pharmaceutical innovation to reach the market, plus another two years or more to reach peak earnings.

facturers in Britain. (The other three are Glaxo, Burroughs Wellcome and ICI: *see table 6*.) The group had had a century of experience in such proprietary medicines as 'Beecham's Pills' when in 1943 its application for a licence to manufacture the newly-discovered antibiotic penicillin was rejected by the government on the grounds of its inexperience of ethical drugs.[1] Another decade went by before the company—still strongly attracted by the burgeoning market for antibiotics—consulted one of the world's great microbiologists, Professor Ernst Chain, who with Fleming and Florey at Oxford had discovered penicillin in the 1930s. Chain suggested the company might carve itself a niche in this market by keeping clear of the massive empirical search for natural antibacterial organisms and concentrating instead on the chemistry of semi-synthetic penicillins.

While Beecham prepared research facilities at Brockham Park, Surrey, for the new quest, two newly recruited company scientists joined Chain in Rome at the Instituto Superiore di Sanità to begin a research project. The scheme was dramatically successful, for inside nine months the recruits and their Italian co-workers had synthesised p-amino benzyl penicillin. It set Beecham firmly on the path to its big semi-synthetic penicillins of the 1960s: Celbenin (which *The Lancet* heralded as 'a major event in chemotherapy'), Orbenin and Penbritin. By 1973 semi-synthetic penicillins were earning about £80 million a year for the organisation.

Penicillin, one of the safest major drugs ever to be discovered, is also one of the very few major pharmaceutical innovations to come originally from academic research. The reason why so few come from this source is not so hard to understand when one considers the size of the scientific effort, in the US and Britain especially, needed to turn the Oxford discovery into the range of penicillin drugs and derivatives we know today. A manufacturer at the innovative end of the drug industry has to be prepared to plunge heavily into scientific resources at whichever point seems to be hindering progress: the physiological, pharmacological, chemical, toxicological, or some other point. No university or other academic institution is ever set up sufficiently flexible for this purpose. It calls for decisions that can be made only under the stimulus of the market place: for a conviction that by organising a concerted scientific assault at some point, perhaps many, a disease problem may be overcome or alleviated from which the sponsors may benefit financially. For the same reason major new drugs are not born of contracts made with contract research organisations.

[1] J. Langrish, 'Innovation in pharmaceuticals', *Research Policy*, vol. 1, 1971–2, pp. 88–9.

What, why, how?

An eminent research director in the pharmaceutical industry once summed up for me industry's attitude to the vast spectrum of science represented by the search for new drugs. 'I want to know *what* a drug will do. *How*, I leave to the universities. *Why*, I leave to the philosophers.'

Even so, discovering what drugs will do—for good or ill—costs the British pharmaceutical industry about £30 million a year (1973). Research expenditure has been rising steeply—more steeply than inflation in this highly labour-intensive activity. A 'Little Neddy' report in 1972 found the rate of growth for the 1960s was about 11·5 per cent per annum at current prices—'substantially faster than the rate of growth of the pharmaceutical market as a whole'.[1] Yet the number of major new drugs to reach the market fell sharply throughout the 1960s. According to *Chemical Insight*, an average of eighty-seven new drugs were marketed each year from 1960 to 1965 in France, Germany, Italy and Britain. During the following six years 1966–71, the annual average fell to fifty-seven new drugs. In 1972 the tally was only forty-three.[2]

The overriding reason is that a major advance in drug research is growing more and more difficult to achieve—simply because there has been so much progress over the past two decades. To quote ICI's director of research: 'Where, twenty years ago, almost every important therapeutic objective remained to be achieved, there are now large numbers of fine drugs for humans and farm animals.'

Dr. Alfred Spinks, a pharmacologist himself, adds that a contributory factor to the decline was the difficulty of designing a compound with a good chance of useful biolgical activity and a small chance of harmful activity. Drug design, he admits, is still a hit-and-miss affair. Fundamental research on disease, on living mechanisms, on drug mechanisms would gradually steer the drug industry towards a more rational and predictive approach to drug design—but that stage has not been reached yet.

Asking the right questions

'The limitation on what you can do has never been money but good ideas', pointed out Sir Alan Wilson, then Glaxo's chairman, in an interview with the *Financial Times* in 1972, just before he retired.[3]

[1] *Focus on Pharmaceuticals*, National Economic Development Office, HMSO, 1972, p. 33.
[2] *Chemical Insight*, no. 41, 1973, p. 5.
[3] David Fishlock, 'Why Glaxo has centralised', the *Financial Times*, 18 October 1972.

Table 6   World's leading pharmaceutical companies in 1972

(courtesy, *Chemical Insight*)

Rank	Company	Sales $m.	Rank	Company	Sales $m.
1	H. la Roche [1]	1,000	26	Dow Chemical [4]	253
2	Am. Home Products	906	26	Schering AG	253
3	Warner Lambert [2]	877	28	*Beecham*	235
4	Merck & Co.	821	29	Smith Kline [1]	229
5	Ciba-Geigy	637	30	Akzo	198
6	Hoechst	593	31	Abbott	192
7	Pfizer	559	32	*ICI*	188
8	Eli Lilly	516	33	*Wellcome* [1]	176
9	Sandoz	481	34	E Merck	134
10	Sterling Drug	460	35	Boots [5]	131
11	Richardson Merrell	457	36	Astra	124
12	Bayer	441	37	Gist Brocades [1]	118
13	Bristol Myers [2]	427	38	Morton-Norwich [2]	115
14	Takeda	422	39	Boehringer-Mannheim	105
15	Squibb	415	40	Miles Labs.	87
16	*Glaxo* [3]	374	41	Fisons	61
17	Schering Plough	360	42	Labaz	52
18	Upjohn	353	42	Nicholas Int.	52
19	Rhone-Poulenc	324	44	UCB	50
20	Boehringer-Ingelheim	297	45	Sumitomo	48
21	Roussel-Uclaf	288	46	Knoll AG	46
22	Johnson & Johnson	283	47	ACF [1]	44
23	Montedison	281	48	Castaigne	38
24	Cyanamid	273	49	Degussa	31
25	Baxter Labs.	254	50	Cafaro	29

Note: Unless stated figures represent pharmaceutical and related products only. All ratings are based on latest annual reports, currencies having been translated to dollars at exchange rates ruling at the end of the respective financial years.

[1] Estimated
[2] Pharmaceuticals plus estimated proportion of pharmaceuticals in international business
[3] Pharmaceuticals and food, less wholesaling
[4] Dow 'bioproducts'
[5] All manufactured goods

Wilson, a physicist, whose own research had earned him election into the Royal Society at the unusually early age of thirty-six, had joined Glaxo—Britain's biggest pharmaceutical group—in 1962 as its director of research. Although group chairman from 1963, he still presided over the two annual meetings of Glaxo's research committee. These two meetings, convened within a couple of weeks of each other, are held (first) to survey the technical aspects of the company's research programme, and (second) to open the research programme to criticism from the company's medical and commercial staffs.

His role at these meetings, Wilson asserted, was simply to ensure that the company's £5 million research programme was fully integrated with all other company activities—'an iterative process', as he saw it. His experience in charge of research for Courtaulds for seventeen years from the end of the war had already convinced him that science could be harnessed efficiently for profit provided management never relaxed in its interest and vigilance of its scientists' activities.

Making sure that the right questions were asked of the scientists was a particular preoccupation with Wilson. He admitted that he deliberately set out to arouse conflict of views between Glaxo's chemists and pharmacologists in the belief that more questions would get answered that way. But he also pointed to the danger of letting the commercial staff pose the wrong questions—and of allowing the research staff to try to answer them. It was his job at the research committee meetings to make sure the right questions were asked—and answered.

The meetings—which antedated Wilson's own appointment—ensured that each person made a personal case for research he wanted or wanted stopped. Wilson, as chairman, saw himself above the battle. 'I'm only interested in research as a means to an end—I'm not emotionally bound up in the projects.' From that vantage point he could also bring other talents to play; as interpreter, for example, between research aspirations and commercial prospects 'It's no good going on about splitting seven-membered rings.'

But it was nevertheless the responsibility of research in a science-based industry to take the initiative, he contended. At Courtaulds, where from very modest beginnings he quickly built up a large research effort, and later with Glaxo he adhered to the principle that if something was agreed to be worth researching the first priority was to get it started, and then to worry about organising it. The decision to start, however, must be soundly based. Only bad decisions are taken when the scientists themselves are doubtful but someone suggests that it may be worth spending a lot of money—just in case. Then, said Wilson, the scientists will spend money instead of thinking.

One of the most important decisions Sir Alan Wilson took on behalf of Glaxo was to use his experience of research and its management to fight off a take-over bid from the Beecham Group in 1971–2. Beecham's directors saw that two companies big in antibiotics, with complementary ranges of food, drink and proprietary medical products would, if merged, be more powerfully placed to meet intense competition from the US, Swiss and German drug companies. Wilson profoundly disagreed. Beecham was a newcomer to drug research with a much narrower range of research targets. Wilson advised the Monopolies Commission that Glaxo's highly successful drug research programme, far from benefiting, might well suffer if coalesced with that of Beecham.

The Monopolies Commission, in a unanimous report, concurred. Success in drug research, it said, depends primarily on the ability to generate novel ideas and on having the resources to develop from those ideas valuable products. There were no grounds for believing a merger would produce more promising ideas—indeed there were grounds for believing it might produce less. 'Our conclusion is that the risks outweigh the possible gains and that the merger would therefore operate against the public interest in its effect on research and development.'[1]

It offered three reasons for this conclusion:

1. The removal of an incentive to Beecham to broaden the scope of its research.
2. The elimination of an important independent centre for deciding the allocation of funds for research and the direction and pattern of research work, which would jeopardise the discovery and development of new products to the British-owned pharmaceutical industry.
3. Damage to the morale of the Glaxo research staff in a merged organisation.

These disadvantages, the Monopolies Commission reported, were of particular significance since the future size and competitiveness of the British-owned pharmaceutical industry and its contribution to the national economy depended heavily upon success in the discovery and development of new products.

Whatever else the report may have achieved or prevented—and it certainly took the City by surprise—it served to highlight the fact that successful research is the bedrock of commercial success in the pharmaceutical business. Its significance here can be equated with the importance of well-managed investment in process plant at the heavier end of the chemical industry.

[1] *The Monopolies Commission Report on the Proposed Mergers of Beecham and Glaxo and Boots and Glaxo*, HMSO, July 1972, pp. 47–59.

Buying into the big league

In the late 1960s ICI, third of Britain's big four in pharmaceuticals but only thirty-second in the world league (*table 6*), took the decision to plunge heavily into drug research—more heavily than anyone else in Britain. It looked at its record for innovation from the 1940s when it discovered the anti-malarial Paludrine to the 1960s when it spawned a series of major new heart drugs. Mr. Reginald Hoare, chairman of ICI's Pharmaceutical Division, and Spinks, then his deputy chairman, believed that the record justified an expansion of research; an attempt, in short, to buy its way much nearer the top of the league table of pharmaceutical companies. They committed the company to spending £100–150 million on drug research and development over the decade 1973–83, once its greatly expanded research facilities at Alderley, Cheshire, came into use.[1] No other division of ICI is spending so heavily on research.

How did Hoare reach such a decision? The research targets, he admits, are growing more difficult to meet—'not fewer but the easier targets have all been scooped up'. The growing body of knowledge of the underlying sciences of pharmacology and toxicology, which brings in its wake increasingly severe regulations, is also making drug research more costly and more hazardous for the businessman. The upshot has been a gradual lengthening of the development time and of the odds against success. The six- or seven-year development period which the drug industry has usually claimed lately is in reality misleadingly low, according to Hoare, who believes it is nearer to ten years. From his own experience with ICI inventions it takes about twelve years from discovery until a new drug has reached peak earnings. (This assertion is worth comparing with the fifteen years estimated for a new aero-engine to reach peak earnings, chapter 3.)

Hoare has no illusions about its being a high-risk business. He confesses to some big disappointments—'more than our share for the rest of the century'. He has had to abandon three drugs in three years. During that period the company launched only one newly synthesised major product, the heart drug Eraldin. One drug abandoned was a highly promising treatment for rheumatic diseases, a sector still rather poorly served by science. At a late stage in the drug's development, when production capacity was being built both in Britain and abroad, it was found to cause jaundice in a few of the women participating in the clinical trials. Hoare immediately called a halt to commercial plans. It took his scientists another year to discover the cause —a basic flaw in the compound—by which time it was clear that the

[1] David Fishlock, 'ICI raises its stake in drugs', the *Financial Times*, 12 October 1973.

painstaking research process must be done all over again. Meanwhile a rival product comparable in efficacy succeeded in reaching the market, raising the hurdle which any new drug must clear for commercial success.

His other drug disappointments have been on the veterinary side of his business, representing some 15 per cent of turnover. In 1972 the research workers found that a new anti-bacterial for infection in chickens had the problem of build-up in drug resistance. The following year Hoare ordered manufacture to cease of a growth promoter for pigs, when long-term studies in rats revealed that after many months of feeding at high dosages the rats tended to develop malignant tumours. The product, then promising a multi-million pound annual market, was promptly dropped, lest it should prove carcinogenic for those who must handle it during its manufacture.

The decision to create a new ICI division for pharmaceuticals was taken by ICI late in the Second World War, but until the late 1950s the research was still carried out by Dyestuffs (now renamed Organics) Division, birthplace of so much ICI innovation. In fact the company was much slower than some of its rivals among the big chemical companies to acknowledge the potential for growth in pharmaceuticals. One reason was that in the early years its drug interests were dominated by tropical diseases, a situation largely dictated by ICI's big post-war operations in India and China. Only gradually was the emphasis shifted away from the tropics with growing appreciation of the importance of hygiene—'it's boots these people want, not drugs' as one cynical scientist puts it. Even then, the shift came not so much from a conscious policy decision but from the need to develop a coherent research programme.

In Hoare's opinion, the planning of a drug research programme implies three things:
1. An assessment of the need for the drug.
2. An estimate of the chances of success.
3. A recognition of the skills available for the search.

The company needs all three. But given the first two, he points out, the third can be attracted.

The basic questions Hoare keeps asking are: 'Is it likely to be important?' and 'Is it likely to be rewarding?' If the answer to either question is 'Yes', then the scientists are given their head. 'But not if it's purely for intellectual reasons.' With those two questions he believes he can prevent a vigorous research effort from becoming dissipated down too many blind alleys.

Most drug companies arrive at their research programme by the same process of reasoning about targets. Generally recognised as desirable but extremely difficult goals, for example, are chemicals that will arrest the various forms of cancer, where leads in recent years have been proved so disappointing that many companies have been reducing their research. Cancer is not a single disease but a great many, sixty or more, each of which will need highly specific treatment for which the market will be small. What is more, it is very unlikely that any drug effective against some form of cancer will be discovered that is not very dangerous itself. Cancer growth is too close in mechanism to normal cell life for it to be otherwise. Another desirable goal is a cure for the common cold, where the overriding problem is to find a drug that is effective yet no more risky or distressing than the disease itself. Where companies will differ in their research programme is in their estimate of the feasibility of a particular objective. This must rest with an estimate of their own resources—which inevitably will be determined by past success.

It was ICI's commercial success in heart drugs in the 1960s, starting with the scientists' discovery of the 'beta-blocking' principle of therapy, that decided Hoare in taking his most profound change in the course of ICI's drug research. 'Here was an area in which hopefully there was a lot of scope for heart and heart-related conditions. It is perhaps our most momentous discovery.' Late in 1968 he swung a big research effort behind cardio-vascular drugs. In the 1970s ICI has been the world's leading supplier of heart drugs—'in sales and in knowledge'—with such drugs as Inderal, Atromid and Eraldin.

How to stop research

Without question the biggest problem in controlling a research programme, in Hoare's opinion, is to stop projects that have outlived their chances of succeeding. The research workers themselves are of little help here. As Walter Marshall, Harwell's research director, has said, 'It is intrinsic to the scientific process that the scientist be motivated to want to do the work and, because he is usually well-motivated, it is usually difficult to stop him doing what he already has in hand to take up something new.' Scientists are always only too ready to assert that the lead they are seeking is just round the corner. Scientists, anyway, are much more inured to disappointments than most professions, but another important factor is that their scientific reputation may be founded on the work they have been doing, quite independently of its chances of commercial success. If the company abandons the quest, and the work fails to find another sponsor such as a university, the scientist may well have to rebuild his name in science from scratch.

Hoare, a pharmacist by training, is acutely sensitive to this problem and the way it can affect one or two key figures behind any research project. His technique is to have his research director put the project on probation for a reasonable period, say a year, stipulating that if, when the year is up, the project is no nearer success it must be abandoned. The uncongenial task of telling the scientists that it must be abandoned is not one he delegates, however, but one he is willing to undertake himself.

CHAPTER 9

Knowing when to stop

'The tendency is for a piece of research to go on till it dies a natural death because of intellectual, leading eventually to financial, inanition.'
Lord Zuckerman, *Beyond the Ivory Tower*

One summer day in 1971 John Williams issued an order closing down British Oxygen's entire central research effort. Newly appointed as chief executive of the £250 million a year industrial gases, metals and chemicals group, Williams—a chemist by training—had decided that his central research effort simply was not paying off.

British Oxygen's corporate research laboratories at Morden in South London had been built up during the late 1960s, chiefly in response to a Monopolies Commission report strongly critical of the company's dominant market position in gases. At the time it was stopped, Dr. John Gardner, research manager, was spending around £300,000 a year in search of new processes and products. But Williams found it was too orientated towards ideas chasing markets and not sufficiently aware of the markets that were going to need new ideas. And in any case the NIH factor ('not invented here') in a company that was not particularly research-conscious tended to make the product divisions resistant to new ideas from central research.

Williams wanted to try a bold new experiment in innovation. He set up instead a small group at headquarters known as the New Venture Secretariat whose objective was not new products or processes but new growth businesses. His idea was that the New Venture Secretariat should take an idea right through to the market and demonstrate it as a business operation before handing it over to a product division.

'I want What Men not Why Men in research,' he told me crisply. 'I want men who ask What is the market? What are the business prospects? not men who ask Why does it work?' He was seeking men with the entrepreneur's instincts but willing to accept the advantages —cash, marketing experience, production skills—a big manufacturing company could offer for somewhat less freedom than venturing alone.

John Williams had one important thing going for him in making his decision to stop central research. He had a challenging new proposal to put to Gardner and some of the staff. A handful of scientists were offered posts in the New Venture Secretariat itself. Meanwhile some of the projects at Morden—superconducting magnet systems, cryogenic refrigeration and industrial electron beams—were considered promising enough to be nursed until ready for exploitation.

A fresh proposition is unquestionably the best way to soften the blow of axing a research project. As the late Dr. Hans Kronberger wrote just before his death in 1970, 'with a good flow of well-justified projects into a laboratory, the main headache of R & D management, namely, how to stop old projects, ceases to exist'.[1]

Kronberger, one of Britain's most brilliant industrial scientists, recognised that rarely would a research manager admit that his laboratory was doing any work that was not essential—'and nowadays he will be able to provide economic analyses to prove his point'. The crucial test, he believed, was to offer the laboratory a new project but no extra staff. If the project were refused it might go to a competing laboratory within the organisation or to a contract laboratory outside. So the research manager would agree—under protest—to put a few people to work assessing the merits of the idea. If satisfied on this score, proposals would usually follow, 'showing how, by further rationalisation of old work in hand, the new job can be handled by his laboratory'.

But what of those economic analyses that showed how essential was the work now being displaced? 'The original economic forecasts can be wrong, and frequently are, and even if they are right, some projects are less valuable than others.' Kronberger knew a laboratory would simply use the less valuable projects to keep staff fully stretched until something better turned up.

One of the harshest realities of the business of science is that successful research is only one of many factors—and not even one of the most crucial factors—in the life-span of a venture in high technology. The most persuasive economic analyses of the merits of a project may be totally irrelevant in the wider context of that project's usefulness and acceptability to society. No economic analysis of the Anglo-French Concorde has the slightest relevance when set against its true purpose—to keep in existence the two great aviation groups British Aircraft Corporation and Aerospatiale, each an important defence contractor.

Dupont's scientists made a great success of their efforts to simulate natural leather with synthetic materials. Corfam 'breathed' just like real leather, through a myriad of minute pores. It kept its finish far better than leather—instead of boot brushes, shoes needed no more

[1] David Fishlock (ed.), *The New Scientists*, Oxford University Press, 1971, p. 25.

than a lick with a damp cloth. It could be made in large rolls where leather arrived in small, cow-shaped fragments. What Dupont's scientists did not anticipate was that fashion changes in the main market for Corfam—female footwear—would introduce an open and thus well-ventilated style of shoe. Much less expensive plastic materials than Corfam could then provide the other advantages of synthetics. Dupont's decision in 1971 to sell off its Corfam operation sealed the fate of what 'must be the most expensive failure in the history of chemical industry', reported *Chemical Age*, 'with its loss estimated at between $80 million and $100 million, a sum which includes research and development costs as well as investment in new plant'.

Scientists themselves—and some of the best at their trade—have often been guilty of deluding themselves and their public with their persuasive 'econo-emotional' cases for the pursuing or sustaining projects irrespective of their usefulness. In an earlier chapter we saw how Professor Eric Laithwaite had beguiled a Parliamentary Select Committee over the hovertrain project, by playing upon public enthusiasm for the 'flying train' concept—a substitute perhaps for the still-lamented steam locomotive, public affection for which was never transferred to its far more efficient diesel and electric successors. By so firmly endorsing the emotional appeal and so totally rejecting the government's case that Tracked Hovercraft was committed to a single, irrelevant course of action, out of touch with any credible market, MPs probably killed any prospect of a new (and much healthier) scheme to use the facilities as a national research centre for very high-speed tracked transport systems. The risk was too great that the misbegotten hovertrain project would simply be hoisted back on the track. (A White Paper published in August 1974 by the Labour government concluded that the decision taken by its predecessors was right.)

A scientific fiasco

An American project that ran amok in a manner that makes the hovertrain project look like exemplary project management was the 'mohole' project of the mid-1960s.[1] Project Mohole has the dubious distinction of being the only basic research project ever to need an Act of Congress to stop it.

As the story is told by Dan Greenberg,[2] Project Mohole was born in 1957, when Dr. Walter Munk, a Californian oceanographer, told a National Science Foundation panel reviewing requests for research

[1] It took its name from the Mohorovicic discontinuity, the interface between crust and mantle beneath the Earth's surface.
[2] *Politics of Pure Science*, New American Library (Plume Book), 1971, p. 170.

grants from earth scientists that, good as the proposals undoubtedly were, none was going to answer a major scientific question about the Earth. What was needed, Munk argued, was a really exciting project to stir the public's imagination and bring fresh blood to geophysics. How about drilling a hole right through the Earth's crust to the mantle beneath?

Munk's idea certainly stirred the scientists' imagination. Samples of the mantle would indisputably answer major questions for geophysics. But getting them called for a hole which on land would be at least nine or ten miles deep—far beyond anything attempted in oil exploration. Even at sea, where the crust can be much thinner, the hole would still need to be more than three miles deep, beneath another three miles of water.

The venture was entrusted to—of all institutions—a society called AMSOC, short for American Miscellaneous Society, founded as a joke a few years before by two geophysicists. It was the antithesis of a traditional scientific society. But AMSOC rose nobly to the challenge, foreswearing its origins; henceforth AMSOC became the name not an abbreviation. It also found headquarters—at the prestigious US Academy of Sciences—along with $15,000 from the National Science Foundation. Project Mohole was on its way. Soon it was able to declare its first estimate of the cost of the project, $5 million, in a case that contained the irresistible argument that 'the ocean's bottom is at least as important to us as the moon's behind'.

For details of the extraordinary escalation in estimated cost of the project that followed I must refer the reader to Greenberg's highly illuminating chapter entitled 'The Anatomy of a Fiasco'. Suffice it to say here that within months the $5 million had been revised upwards to $14 million; and inside three years the estimate had zoomed to $35 million–$50 million. When finally axed in 1966, ten years after Munk first proposed the venture, Project Mohole was expected to need at least $125 million. Long before this, however, the sums had soared far beyond the managerial capacity of an incredibly makeshift scientific administration, to levels where it represented very big business for the embryonic industry of ocean engineering. From that point onwards the venture—as a serious project of basic science—was probably doomed. Industry and politics took control; and industry's interest in such a project must lie in what further business might follow; an interest that was not going to be served by a single successful penetration of the Earth's crust.

In the early 1960s Dan Greenberg,[1] one of the most perceptive

[1] Greenberg spent two years, 1969–70, in Britain as European editor of *Science*, but admits he returned to the US little wiser about the mechanisms by which the British reached their decisions in scientific and technological affairs.

commentators on the politics of science and technology, created the character of Dr. Grant Swinger—the outcome of an allegedly scientific conference he had attended and found, in his own words, to be 'pure bullshit'. Dr. Grant Swinger epitomised a new attitude infiltrating the politics of science, in which the supplicant for research support expanded his case far beyond the logic of science. He would not hesitate to hint of untold commercial or sociological benefits beyond his immediate proposal, or—as with Project Mohole—of some fiendish plot by a hostile nation to get the information first. In the past decade or so Grant Swinger has successively espoused the causes of space science, military research, environmental science and, just lately, energy research. His ubiquity and growing political skills have made it increasingly hard for anyone to take a detached and dispassionate view of the merits of any given project, and thus to know when the time has come to cry 'Stop!'.

Cure for cancer

'Don't let's fool ourselves' was one of the favourite phrases at meetings of Solly Zuckerman, chief scientific adviser to the British government from 1964 until his retirement in 1971, and even then an *eminence grise* in the Cabinet Office. The phrase usually presaged some unpalatable truth. An arrogant man but one of great humility in face of facts is how a colleague recalls him from the salad days of the 1960s when, as chief scientific adviser to the Ministry of Defence, he was effectively in control of one third of the nation's entire research budget. His impatience with civil servants was a byword in Whitehall. 'God knows, I'm arrogant—but he *knows*', he once said exasperatedly of some mandarin.

Shortly after his retirement in 1971 the Prime Minister asked Zuckerman to report on cancer research in Britain. President Nixon had announced a national campaign to conquer cancer, backed by a big increase in federal funds for research. Was there a case for doing so in Britain?

During the 'fifties and 'sixties such a request of the scientific community would have been the signal for a persuasively argued case backed by economic analyses for making a thumping great increase in research support. But Prime Minister Heath had picked for the task not a committee of experts, but a scientist well versed in the efforts of two successive governments to gain some control over the research process and the deployment of research resources; and one, moreover, with a reputation for bringing intellectual honesty to bear where it was lacking before. Lord Zuckerman's report in October 1972 was a great disappointment to some sectors of the scientific community. He found that cancer was probably costing the nation about £80 million a year in direct costs, against which research—mostly charity-funded—was costing £10 million a year. In other words, even by high technology standards Britain was already spending heavily on cancer research. He concluded that 'with certain exceptions, a sudden increase in funds for cancer research could not be effectively used'. But a 'steady and substantial increase over the years would probably yield valuable results, at least in terms of producing a coherent scientific programme'.[1] The conclusion was much too downbeat in tone for the *New Scientist*, for example, which argued in an editorial that 'as the story of discoveries made under the pressures of wartime necessity show, innovation and research *can* be hastened. In the context of cancer research this means that while lavish investment can never guarantee returns, it does increase the chances of successful pay-off.'[2] The journal did not venture an estimate of what level of 'lavish investment' in cancer research it thought justified by the magnitude of the problem.

The fallacy in the *New Scientist*'s case was that, while it is well established that pressures of war can accelerate the *application* of discoveries, there is little or no evidence that they hasten the progress of scientific understanding and discovery. The basic discoveries that led to the great technical advances of the Second World War, such as atomic energy, rockets, jet engines, radar, antibiotics, antimalarials and nerve poisons, had all been made before the war, sometimes long before. This was the fallacy that led Britain, in company with other industrial nations, to set up big national laboratories with lavish funding after the war, in the belief that they could hustle science along. At best they have hustled development and application along. In the case of cancer there is nothing waiting to be hustled along. The basic scientific understanding that might be turned into useful therapies by, say, the drug industry is still missing. A naïve popular belief that given enough cash, scientist can solve any problem is no longer shared by the drug industry, despite the obvious commercial appeal of finding a 'cure for cancer'. Companies, disillusioned, are now cutting back hard from what in some cases were quite high levels of investment in the late 1960s.

In *Beyond the Ivory Tower* Zuckerman admits frankly that he doubts whether close correspondence could ever be achieved between social needs and the deployment of technological resources. 'There will always be differences of view about social priorities; while the inevitable set-backs that occur in the course of the evolution of a technological project can be relied upon to separate conception from

[1] *Cancer Research*, a report by Lord Zuckerman, HMSO, 1972.
[2] *New Scientist*, 2 November 1972.

achievement, and to disrupt carefully laid plans, however well conceived in relation to desirable social needs.'[1] But he finds signs 'however vague' that the pattern of deployment of scientific resources is 'beginning to move gradually in a direction which accords more closely with some broadly conceived view of the way they should be deployed in the best interests not only of society's present, but also future well-being.' Zuckerman cites, for example, the way that the national budget for defence research and development has fallen as a proportion of the government's research expenditure, from about 70 per cent in 1958–9 to 43 per cent in 1969–70. Elsewhere I have cited the efforts of the Science Research Council to reduce the proportion of funds devoted to high-energy physics. In each case the change has inevitably been slow—in the one because of the sheer size and political clout of the defence research establishment, and in the other because of the immense cost of the instruments and facilities needed to keep the science progressing.

But how should resources released by such changes be redeployed? On cancer research—when the evidence so overwhelmingly is that so much cancer is self-inflicted by cigarette smoking? On safer vehicles—when the evidence is that technological advances simply encourage drivers to take greater risks? On public transport—when the public has been brain-washed to think that very fast trains are the answer while the real delays and frustrations are in urban transportation?

Principle of maximum unfairness

In a tavern a few miles from Harwell in Berkshire I got my first briefing on the efforts being made by the British government to re-align the nation's research effort. It was late in 1967, soon after I joined the *Financial Times*. That summer the Labour government had announced a savage cut in future funds for research on nuclear fusion, the budget for which was to be reduced from £5 million to £2·5 million over the ensuing five years. The reason was that the fusion physicists could make no plausible case for claiming that a fusion power source was within reach. A mutual friend introduced me to Walter Marshall, who lost no time in letting me know that his opinion of newspaper reporting of science's activities was pretty poor. An outstanding scientist whose own researches in plasma and solid-state physics earned him election into the Royal Society while still in his thirties, he expected reports and comments on science topics to reflect more of the rigours of logic and precision of science.

The story Marshall unfolded at dinner that night and soon after

[1] Solly Zuckerman, *Beyond the Ivory Tower*, Weidenfeld and Nicolson, 1970.

at Harwell was concerned not with 'breakthroughs' but rather survival. Harwell and the nearby Culham laboratory (where work on nuclear fusion was carried out) together formed the research group of the UK Atomic Energy Authority. Its job was to provide the more fundamental physics and chemistry needed by the reactor engineering and nuclear fuel laboratories at Risley, Dounreay and elsewhere, and the nuclear weapons factory at Aldermaston. For several years it had been clear that with the greater part of this mission very successfully accomplished, a new role must be found to justify a research effort involving over 6,000 staff. More recently it had also become clear that fusion was not ready to provide a new mission—indeed that it did not then warrant even the existing effort.

The most obvious course of action would be to cut the research group back to a size commensurate with the mission remaining, which meant to one-third of its size. It would release a great deal of technical talent for industry to redeploy. The government had one important reservation about this course of action—that the scientists and engineers who had helped to make Harwell one of the world's great research centres were not going to be bought up by those very industries, such as the mechanical engineering industries, most urgently in need of the services of science. Marshall and his colleagues had another reservation—that a Harwell shrunk to one-third of its size would simply not be up to its very demanding nuclear energy tasks, concerned increasingly with the fast reactor. So many questions remained that no one could be sure, when problems arose, which of Harwell's vast array of techniques and talent would be needed for 'fire brigade' action. (The point was well made a few years later when a problem that threatened to arrest the £45 million prototype fast reactor project yielded to studies with one of Harwell's atom smashers.)

It was Harwell's idea that the laboratory should be given a new national mission; one attuned to the government's preoccupation with poor economic performance, and particularly the nation's failure to exploit innovation successfully. The government, well aware that Harwell was only the first of a number of national research centres whose missions were drawing to an end, was well disposed towards the Harwell solution. It even endorsed the idea that Harwell should flout all traditions of British government science and instead of making results freely available to all-comers (as taxpayers), it should work exclusively on the development and exploitation of high technology with chosen industrial partners. With characteristic irreverence the idea was christened the 'principle of maximum unfairness'.

What Marshall and his colleagues were proposing was to turn Harwell into a national contract research centre, capable of generating ideas of its own for which it would seek exclusive commercial partners for exploitation, and also willing to undertake industry's problems in sectors where it had some experience. At the same time it would have a large bedrock of nuclear research. It would judge its performance by its earnings—by what industry, government and overseas customers could be persuaded to pay for work beyond its brief for the UK Atomic Energy Authority. The argument here was quite straightforward. As Marshall puts it,

> Our new mission made sense only if we made a genuine contribution to help industry. If we made a genuine contribution then we would help industry to earn more money and, if they earned more money, they ought to be prepared to pay us for our help. On the other hand, if they were not prepared to pay us for our research we were probably misorienting our efforts.

Given the green light in 1967 by Mr. Anthony Wedgwood Benn, Minister of Technology, Harwell promptly embarked on its new career as a contract research organisation. British industry, never enthusiastic about contract research, was positively hostile towards the laboratory's intentions. In *The New Scientists* Marshall spells out no less than eighteen obstacles, mostly raised by industry, ranging from the high cost of overheads at Harwell to its inexperience of the market place.[1] One of the most telling points was that the scheme was simply not credible financially. To earn a third of its income—say £4–5 million a year at 1967 prices—from private industry implied being associated with industries commanding a turnover of £500 million a year. It also implied that Harwell must earn more than any other contract research organisation this side of the Atlantic.

But by the early 1970s the laboratory had caught up in earnings with the biggest of Europe's contract research organisations (*see table 7*).

Table 7 Income of Europe's biggest research contractors, 1972–73

	£m.
Battelle—Geneva	6·5
Battelle—Frankfurt	5·8
Huntingdon Research Centre	3·8
International Research and Development (IRD)	1·25
Harwell	4·8

At Harwell, in Whitehall and among the laboratory's industrial customers and collaborators I find a quite astonishing unanimity of

[1] Walter Marshall, 'Harwell Changes Course', *The New Scientists*, Oxford University Press, 1971, p. 55.

E

opinion that the man primarily responsible for this success is no professional salesman but a theoretical physicist who enjoys nothing better than his annual sabbatical in some research centre overseas when he can get back to his mathematics. Of Marshall, Dr. Alvin Weinberg, then director of the Oak Ridge National Laboratory, one of America's most famous research centres, said to me some years ago, 'Had he stayed around here much longer I think he would have taken us over.'

Every few weeks a handful of seasoned scientists from Marshall's staff spend three days at the Oxford Centre for Management Studies a few miles from Harwell, where they learn the rudiments of marketing strategy and tactics. The big lesson that Marshall preaches and the Centre reinforces is that marketing research can be a rewarding and exciting extension of the research process itself. It is a lesson his staff has taken to heart for by 1973 Harwell had sold its services to well over a hundred industrial companies, including some of Britain's biggest spenders in research and—perhaps more significantly—some with little or no experience of the value of science.

'We set out,' says Dr. Freddie Clarke, marketing director, highly regarded as a materials scientist when he turned to marketing at the start of Harwell's new career, 'believing that we might sell ceramics technology to the ceramics industry, chemical engineering to the chemical industry, and so on.' It did not work that way. A high proportion of the research effort Clarke markets goes to quite disparate industries—ceramics technology for the motor car industry, heat transfer technology for the food processing industry, computer technology for the sea transport industry. Clarke, conscious of the dangers for Harwell of 'trying to ride off in all directions', hammers home the lesson that there are a small number of industries —electrical, mechanical and instrument engineering, ceramics, textiles and chemicals—on which his research managers must concentrate, while keeping watch for any industry that suddenly decided to expand its research investment (as the food, drink and tobacco industries have done).

Exit carbon fibre

Marshall makes no secret, however, that there have been some big disappointments and some harsh lessons learned from the experience of getting 'deeply immersed in the commercial and industrial life of the country'. Harwell developed a range of nuclear-powered batteries for remote applications, such as transmitters or beacons on the seabed or mountaintop, but could find no commercial partner. It developed a new method of desalinating seawater by freezing that was economically promising—but not quite promising enough to warrant the expense of a large-scale demonstration. But carbon fibre provided one of the biggest disappointments.

When the Harwell experiment began, carbon fibre was near the top of the list of high technologies it believed it could exploit profitably. At an early stage of the invention of carbon fibre of high strength and stiffness by scientists at Farnborough, Harwell's experience of graphite technology was harnessed to scale up the Farnborough process. For many months Harwell was the source of the carbon fibre Rolls-Royce was using to reinforce experimental plastic aero-engine components, following Lombard's decision to incorporate the new material into his design for a big engine (*see chapter 3*).

Marshall and his colleagues became convinced that, so remarkable were the properties of the new carbon fibre 'composite' materials, herein lay a chance of giving a break not just to aviation but to the British engineering industries generally. Relatively small amounts of the fibre could upgrade all manner of engineering products, leading to machines and structures that were stronger or quicker or lighter. It was reinforced in this view by the enthusiasm shown by ICI, which had ideas for a major new business operation based on supplying composite materials, with carbon fibre materials at the premium end of the range.

There was one small problem. To honour promises made to two companies—Courtaulds and Morgan Crucible—brought in by Farnborough in the earliest stages of its carbon fibre development programme, the National Research Development Corporation had granted both companies licences for manufacture under the Farnborough patents. Each had plans for a small pilot carbon fibre plant making a few tons a year, aimed primarily at the aero-space market, with a product selling for upwards of £80 a pound. Neither company shared Harwell's confidence of finding a much bigger market quickly; both were opposed to the ICI plan.

At ICI's request, Harwell designed a carbon fibre plant with a much bigger output, 500 tons a year. Such a plant, it believed, could make carbon fibre at a price attractive to many industries other than aerospace. Thus Harwell hoped to concertina the long slow process by which a novel material developed for some high technology purpose gradually expands in application as its properties become more widely understood and appreciated and production costs fall. The high-nickel (Nimonic) alloys and titanium alloys are prime examples of this protracted process of introducing a new material to engineering.

Harwell's conviction that it could 'buck the system' was founded above all on two counts. One was the prestige of Rolls-Royce and the importance the company was publicly attaching to carbon fibre for the success of its RB.211 project. The other count was that a carbon fibre plant of 500 tons annual output could manufacture fibre for about £5 per pound—at which price it would find a market for its output. It foundered on count two. A high-powered market survey undertaken by ICI at a cost of £250,000, in which Harwell participated fully, disclosed that so inherently costly were the very high temperature processes needed to make carbon fibre, in order to justify a selling price of £5 per pound the initial market must be upwards of 2,000 tons. An initial market of this size just was not credible. Even Rolls-Royce, before it dropped carbon fibre in 1970, expected to need no more than tens of tons a year. ICI decided in 1969 not to proceed with its plans. Marshall, deeply disappointed, agreed nonetheless that he could find no fault with a decision so firmly founded on the principles he himself was preaching about bringing the deductive logic of science into business.

Harwell still has a research programme on carbon fibre applications, including work on carbon fibre gas centrifuge rotors (chapter 11), a problem similar in many respects to the RB.211 fan blade. In 1973–4 its customers spent about £120,000 on these applications. The British invention will follow the traditional long bumpy trail for a novel engineering material in slowly winning acceptance among designers—who in turn will be wondering if a bold decision like Rolls-Royce's could bring them the same fate.

Such setbacks notwithstanding, it became plain that both the Labour government that authorised the Harwell experiment, and the Tory government that initially was rather hostile, were delighted with progress overall. The Labour government in its last year of office extrapolated Harwell's success into a scheme for achieving close correspondence between social needs and the deployment of technological resources. In a Green Paper early in 1970 it proposed a merging of ten national laboratories and the National Research Development Corporation into a single research agency, the British Research and Development Corporation. This agency would have a budget of £60–70 million (at 1970 prices), which after five years or so of operations would derive equally from three sources: parliamentary vote (for 'basic' research, standards, and so on), research contracts placed by government departments and research contracts placed by British and overseas industry.

The British Research and Development Corporation proposal was criticised chiefly for being 'absurdly optimistic' in its estimates of what industry might be persuaded to spend on contract research, when in the past it had shown so little enthusiasm either for the contract research laboratories already existing or for using the services available (free) from such national laboratories as the

National Engineering Laboratory. Yet by 1973–4 Harwell alone was securing contracts worth around £7 million from the industrial sector. Other laboratories of the UK Atomic Energy Authority brought the tally to some £10 million.

Enter Rothschild

The real weakness of the proposal for a British Research and Development Corporation was not the optimism of its estimates of industrial support—although Marshall himself warns that Harwell's experience should not be used as an exact model for other laboratories—or even its relatively cumbersome structure. Its real weakness was that, big though the agency would be, it would attempt to deal with only part of the problem of closer correspondence between national needs and national research resources—and not necessarily the most urgent part. It would scarcely touch the problems of the health service, the agricultural community or the broad sector concerned with the 'environment' (which includes transport, construction and city development).

In the summer of 1970 a Conservative government led by Mr. Heath took office. There followed some swift changes in Whitehall. Mintech, authors of the British Research Development Corporation proposal, was merged with the Board of Trade, creating the huge Department of Trade and Industry. Another 'superministry' called the Department of the Environment was formed from such backwater departments as transport, housing and public buildings and works.

More important than either in this context, however, was the creation by Mr. Heath of the Central Policy Review Staff, as his own personal sensory mechanism to monitor the performance of government. Set up in the Cabinet Office, independent of any departmental responsibility, the 'think tank' as it soon became known was something quite new in British government. It brought into the Cabinet Office the uncompromising figure of Lord Rothschild. And so it came to pass that for the next few years Rothschild—a biophysicist who once studied the sex life of sea urchins—became the most widely quoted name in British science.

CHAPTER 10

Getting control of research

'The needs of our country are too important, urgent and identifiable to rely on chance discoveries—to warrant those needs being left to a form of scientific roulette in which there are many more numbers for the ball to enter than the conventional 37.'

Lord Rothschild, 1971

Victor Rothschild is a big, burly fellow with a refreshingly salty turn of phrase for so autocratic a presence. But he swears deliberately to spice the point he is making, whether it is a carefully considered opinion of some aspect of government strategy or an impromptu piece of character assassination. He smiles very little yet has immense charm to temper the authority he carries so convincingly. He has enough disrespect for the System, however, to relish the story of the first approach from the Prime Minister about a job in the Cabinet Office, at the head of the proposed Central Policy Review Staff, or 'think tank'. He was on the point of retiring from Shell and largely preoccupied with the usual round of farewell parties, when Sir Burke Trend, then secretary to the Cabinet, called to offer the new job. But Rothschild's secretary barred the way, saying her master was much too busy at present to be interrupted.

The new job in Whitehall placed a scientist in much closer communication with the Prime Minister than had been the case in Britain since the Second World War. From 1964 Zuckerman was officially appointed the first chief scientific adviser to the government, having served unofficially in that capacity for some years before. But the purpose of the appointment was to have a scientist's opinion 'on tap', not as part of the decision-making process in government. It gave neither Zuckerman nor his successor, Sir Alan Cottrell, the access Rothschild enjoyed, which it has been said placed him among the four top civil servants of the early 1970s, along with Trend[1] himself, Sir William Armstrong, head of the Civil Service Department, and Sir Douglas Allen of the Treasury.

Rothschild believes he was offered the job because he had a rather unusual combination of academic and industrial experience of science. From 1950 to 1970 he held the post of assistant director

[1] Sir Burke Trend, now Lord Trend, retired in September 1973.

of research in the Department of Zoology at Cambridge. From 1961 he was also director of research for the Royal Dutch-Shell Group. Shell is among the most research conscious of companies, spending over £70 million annually on research and development and willing to fund research at an unusually basic level. At one stage the company boasted no less than five Fellows of the Royal Society. One of the first jobs the Prime Minister tossed to the 'think tank' was one with which Rothschild had already wrestled for ten years at Shell: how to make a big research effort responsive to the patron's needs. In this case, however, the patron was the taxpayer, faced with a bill for government science exceeding £750 million a year.

As I have tried to show in earlier chapters, the research process has a will of its own, and a strong one at that. The tendency all the time is for established lines of research to expand and fan out, ever absorbing more and more effort—which since research is a very labour-intensive activity means more and more cash. It is very much easier to increase the effort in an established direction than to change the direction. It is still harder to induce good scientists in the more academic reaches of science to turn their minds to problems they see as unfashionable—no matter how compelling a case one makes for finding solutions. The scientists' answer is simply that, if enough cash is offered, someone else will be induced to work on the problem.

Successive governments had seen the problem a little differently, however. They saw an urgent need to prise loose at least a little of the cash they were already spending for the study of a few problems— in health, agriculture, transport, crime, and so on—that were causing the public genuine concern.

Customer–contractor relationship

It took the 'think tank' six months to produce the 'Rothschild Report'.[1] Its publication in November 1971 produced a public reaction from the world of science of a vehemence unknown ever before. Over 200 letters were published in the daily newspapers and science Press. 'A threat to the well-being of British science which must be resisted', wrote one protester. It was a pretty fair summary of the feelings of most of the correspondents, which in turn was reflected in editorial opinion in most of the papers. (Exceptions were *Nature* and the *Financial Times*.) A stern warning came from the President of the Royal Society, Professor Alan Hodgkin—another Cambridge biophysicist and close friend of Rothschild—of the dangers of disrupting research with the Rothschild plan. Any nation with a 'reasonably satisfactory' method of supporting science should think very carefully

[1] *A Framework for Government Research and Development*, Cmnd. 4184, HMSO, 1971.

before dismantling it, he believed.[1] So deep ran their feelings that the two friends made a pact never again to discuss the plan themselves.

What manner of plan could prompt so violent a response from so docile a sector of society as science? Rothschild's report had been terse—a mere 25 pages—but it packed in a total of fifty-five recommendations. The protesters' fury focused, however, on a very commercial sounding phrase, the 'customer–contractor relationship'. Such a relationship, said the report, should replace the scientist's complete freedom to do work of his own choosing for a substantial amount of government-funded research.

Rothschild's own definition of 'customer–contractor relationship' is itself an excellent example of the economy of words that characterises his report: 'The customer says what he wants; the contractor does it (if he can); and the customer pays.' It was a principle already firmly established in one huge sector of British science, defence research, which accounted for about half of the government's outlay on research.

Scientific research is really an attempt to fashion the future, whether its purpose is to strengthen defences, increase the size of the harvest, curb social ills from bronchitis to crime or just to seek new knowledge. A good research centre is not just a place where original discoveries and ideas are developed, but also an intelligence centre equipped to appreciate the significance of discoveries and advances made elsewhere. As we have seen in the case of defence research (chapter 5), strong links with a powerful research team provide departments of government with the skills necessary for looking to the future with confidence. Yet several large sectors of Whitehall, whose activities one might reasonably assume to be taking fullest advantage of scientific enquiry, were found by Rothschild to be making scant use of the nation's research resources. The criticism applied above all to two departments, Health and Agriculture, neither of which had seen fit to spend very much on research themselves.

Thus Rothschild defined the problem of correspondence between research effort and social needs in much broader terms than had Mintech in proposing the British Research and Development Corporation two years before. He was faced with the following choice. He could suggest that the departments deprived of science should start building up new research teams from scratch on a scale commensurate with the size of their budgets. This would delight the science community but was bound to be expensive and very slow; industry reckons it takes seven years or more for a new research centre at a reasonably basic level to contribute anything to its profits. It would also inevitably weaken existing research centres in

[1] The *Financial Times*, 1 December 1971.

Britain, such as those of the Medical Research Council (spending £22·4 million in 1971–2) and the Agricultural Research Council (£18·7 million). In short, it was not at all the sort of solution the government had in mind.

On the other hand, Rothschild could find a way of making the existing research centres more responsive to departmental needs. Once chairman himself of the Agricultural Research Council, he knew well the problems of trying to interest its scientists in the technically tricky problems of applying the basic knowledge of animal and crop diseases to the highly fragmented British agricultural industry. Yet, as he once remarked, 'They have two different laboratories researching apples. I grow apples myself but two can only produce a glut.' Precisely the same circumstances prevailed, he discovered, with human diseases. The Medical Research Council found the problems of vaccination, arthritis and mental diseases too unfashionable for their attention. A study by the 'think tank' of hospital bed occupancy in Britain—the hospital service accounts for half the £2,200 million (1972) budget of the National Health Service —revealed no correspondence between occupancy and the research programme of the Medical Research Council.

In the case of the Agricultural Research Council, the grumblings of the ministry and the farmers themselves had already led to two studies—one by the ministry saying that the research council should be transferred to its control, and the second, an independent study of the research councils by Professor Sir Frederick Dainton, one of the most highly respected of British science policy makers. Dainton's lengthy and elegantly argued report came out firmly against any interference with the autonomy of the Agricultural Research Council. He warned of the risks for government of incensing the science community and losing its co-operation. He based his conclusions on the premise that 'science is a unity and . . . could only suffer by fragmentation corresponding to the responsibilities of different executive departments . . .'. He therefore sought ways of unifying rather than dividing the research councils' work. He allowed for the 'possibility of adjustments of responsibility between the research councils and the transfer of specific activities both into and out of their field'.

Rothschild knew his fellow scientists well enough, however, to know that sweet reason could never achieve any profound change in the situation he had uncovered. The gulf between the mandarins of these two research councils and their corresponding ministries was too great. Each research council held the ministry's scientists largely in contempt. His own report has all the hallmarks of a calculated attempt to stir up the science community. It was also his own idea that the sweetly reasoned case of Dainton for leaving the research councils alone should be juxtaposed in the final publication with his own case for getting—to use a phrase of P. G. Wodehouse—into their ribs with a pole. The government published the two reports as a Green Paper—a document for discussion—in which it was made plain that it favoured Lord Rothschild's plan.

The plan, and the tacit government support, had the desired effect. It provoked a public debate about science policy of unprecedented proportions and sometimes of a venom that made even Rothschild himself think he might have overplayed his hand. As a consequence the Cabinet Office was showered with advice (including over 400 letters and no fewer than four reports from the Select Committee on Science and Technology).

In essence the plan called for the 'customer–contractor relationship' to be applied throughout government-funded science. Large portions of the budgets of three research councils—Medical, Agricultural and Environmental—should be transferred to the control of the relevant government department, which would thus have a direct influence over the applied research programme. (The Science Research Council was exempted—for some years its chairman, Professor Sir Brian Flowers, had been busily building bridges to Mintech, forerunner of the Department of Trade and Industry, chapter 5.) This direct influence would be exercised through a departmental chief scientist and secretariat, just as it already was at the Department of Defence and the Department of Trade and Industry. But an average of about 10 per cent of the research budgets of all government laboratories, Rothschild recommended, should be kept free from control by the customer–contractor relationship, to be spent on basic research—as was already done in Defence.

Who decides?

Terse and to the point as Rothschild's original report was, it soon became clear that he could argue his case as persuasively as Dainton. In a lecture to the Royal Society of Arts he expanded his plan with what the *New Statesman* called 'a quite unfair degree of elegance and wit'. Basic research, he said, was done solely to increase human knowledge. Practically speaking, it was 'useless'—often motivated only by the curiosity of the research worker or his boss.

> If he or she is good—and in spite of the occasional clanger, I think we have reasonable yardsticks to make the measurements to justify such an assertion—we must let them go on, even if, to some of us, the things about which they are inquisitive seem remote, strange, incomprehensible, out of this world and, indeed, out of all other worlds, for that matter.

He added that within the limits of the cash available, the choice of subjects for basic research could be left to the discretion of scientists themselves.

But this could not be so for the very much bigger sector of science known as applied research and development—accounting for 83–87 per cent of government science funds. Although indistinguishable from basic research in how it was done, applied research and development differed in why it was done and who wanted it done.

> The research worker should *not* formulate the objective, though he can and should help. The research worker should *not* decide that the objective requires research for its achievement. He should *not* decide that the research should be done, assuming it is necessary. He should *not* decide when to stop. Nor should he decide to change the objective in mid-stream, however desirable it may seem to him to do so.

Rothschild concluded that a substantial portion of the research programme of the Agricultural Research Council, and smaller portions of the research programmes of the Medical Research Council and the Natural Environment Research Council fell into the category of applied research and development. He proposed that control for these applied portions should be transferred to the relevant government department. The government department would thus become a 'customer' which decided what problems were and were not worth an attempted solution at the taxpayer's expense.

For Flowers the Rothschild plan posed a pretty dilemma. Unquestionably the research council chairman of greatest personal stature, as well as the one with the biggest research budget (*see table 8*), he was highly sympathetic towards both Rothschild's and Dainton's points of view. He alone among research council chairmen had had the foresight back in the mid-1960s to recognise that the boom period in growth of research council budgets could not last, and that his own research council must not remain isolated from the government department—Mintech—likely to make greatest use of its science. But a point of weakness of the Rothschild plan, he told me soon after the Green Paper was published, was the crucial role of the departmental chief scientists. It called for men of exceptional talent who could define clearly what problems the department wanted to try to solve and which stood a fair chance of yielding to a research project. No scientist of sufficient standing in the world of science was going to be persuaded to take on such a task. Yet only eighteen months later another eminent research director, Professor Kenneth Mellanby, director of the Nature Conservancy's Monks Wood Experimental Station, was saying that so impressive were the credentials of the

newly-appointed chief scientists that science itself would be the loser
by their absence from the laboratory.[1]

Table 8   Research Council budgets, 1971–2

	Amounts to be transferred (at 1971–2 prices)			
	£m.	73–4	74–5	75–6
Science Research Council	50·9	Nil	Nil	Nil
Medical Research Council	22·4	2·75	4·25	5·50
Agricultural Research Council	18·7	5·00	7·50	10·00
Natural Environment Research Council	15·3	2·25	3·25	4·50
Social Sciences Research Council	2·2			
TOTAL	109·5	10·00	15·00	20·00

So overwhelmingly opposed to the Rothschild plan was the great
majority of published correspondence that it was easy to get the impression that Dainton was right, after all, and so great an upheaval
as was proposed in research control must surely alienate the scientists
themselves. Closer inspection, though, revealed anomalies in the
pattern of correspondence. Predominantly it came from the medical
scientists and from the medical profession itself; although Rothschild had proposed the transfer of only 25 per cent of Medical
Research Council funds to the control of the Department of Health.
(Rothschild, incidentally, had his own file of correspondence from
research council staff saying, in effect, the plan must go through.)

Virtually unheard was the voice of the far bigger sector of government financed science represented by the laboratories directly controlled by departments of government. Also virtually unheard was
the voice of industrial science which, as my own enquiries at the time
indicated, saw little relevance to their own activities in what appeared
to be a debate among dons. Yet in the spring of 1972, while the
debate was still raging, a meeting in Paris of EIRMA, the European
Industrial Research Management Association, attended by 120 industrial research chiefs from companies throughout Europe, concluded that industry must more closely integrate its scientific and
business planning 'to ensure the optimum use of all resources, and to
ensure that it is properly aware of the pressing needs of society as a
whole'.[2] In other words, the industrial research directors were

---

[1] British Association Lecture, reported in the *New Scientist*, 23 August 1973,
pp. 434–6.
[2] David Fishlock, 'Is science slipping back to normal?', the *Financial Times*,
25 April 1972.

acknowledging that in research and development industry faced precisely the same problems as government in the 1970s. They, too, were turning increasingly to a 'customer–contractor relationship' with contract research centres. Contract research in such sectors as toxicology, mineral exploitation, process technology and transport engineering was enjoying an unprecedented boom. Some companies even began to adapt the customer–contractor principle to the control of research and development within their own laboratories.

Late in the debate came support from a quarter which, if surprising, was one that knew the situation only too well. Mr. Anthony Wedgwood Benn, who as Minister of Technology in the previous government had sired his own departmental solution in the shape of the still-born British Research and Development Corporation, predicted that the customer–contractor principle for the control of applied research and development would 'survive in some form, in whatever organisation emerges'. Once the dust had settled, Rothschild would be:

seen as having been the trigger mechanism for a process of democratisation that goes far beyond the customer-contractor principle which caused such an uproar. Whatever the ultimate outcome of his report, he will be remembered as the man who lifted the lid off the private world of decision-making and did it in such vivid and abrasive language that a lot of other people will now be taking a great deal more interest in everything that happens there.[1]

New look for science

It had also been Lord Rothschild's advice to the Prime Minister that his plan could not be implemented overnight—that too many changes were required, many of which 'will involve changes in attitude, orientation and procedure which will take time to accept, let alone to digest'. How they might be made should be referred to the government's chief scientific adviser, Sir Alan Cottrell.

The final form of the plan appeared in July 1972.[2] For its more implacable opponents it confirmed their worst fears by adhering closely to the original report. For more dispassionate observers, however, Cottrell had made some significant concessions, most obviously in the amount of research council funds to be transferred to departmental control (£20 million: only about 70 per cent of the original recommendations) and in the rate at which the transfer

[1] Anthony Wedgwood Benn, 'For science open government has arrived', *New Scientist*, 11 May 1972, pp. 314–16.
[2] *Framework for Government Research and Development*, Cmnd. 5046, HMSO, 1972.

would be made over a three-year period (*see table 8*). More subtle but more significant, however, was the elaborate system of safeguards, designed to guarantee the right of appeal should either customer or contractor feel aggrieved at the rejection, respectively, of its requests, proposals or its advice. To quote *Nature*, the premier journal of record and comment on science, the White Paper—'sober, perceptive and intelligent'—could with luck become a better framework for the organisation of British science than had existed for several years.[1]

Above all the White Paper made it crystal clear, where Roths-child's report itself perhaps had not, that the government was con-cerned with the direction of the whole of the publicly funded sector of applied research and development, not merely the 10 per cent or less spent by the research councils. It happened, however, that the research councils controlled some national laboratories whose talents and experience were particularly relevant to some of the problems the government considered most urgently in need of solution. This was especially so in the case of sickness—of human, animal and plant diseases.

Sexy research

Science, no less than most other facets of human activity, is very vulnerable to the dictates of fashion. No one has yet discovered a formula for picking winners in science, whether the goal is a Nobel Prize or an entrepreneur's fortune. And common sense tells us that no one is likely to. The usual formula is to try to pick problems be-lieved to be difficult enough to leave one clearly ahead of the compe-tition if the research should have a successful outcome, yet not so difficult that the cost or the time-scale is too forbidding.

The upshot of this highly pragmatic approach is that some sectors of scientific research are considered sexy (so everyone has a go) and some are not; and therein lies one of the basic problems of trying to manage a nation's research and development effort. All too often the problems that are costing a nation dearly, whether in hard cash or distress, are scientifically unsexy and tend to be shunned if the scien-tists are given complete freedom of choice.

In earlier chapters I have given many examples of what might be called sexy research and development financed since the Second World War by the British taxpayer: Concorde, hovercraft and hover-trains, nuclear fusion, atom smashing (these five ventures alone have cost Britain upwards of £600 million on research and develop-ment, for what return I must leave the reader himself to judge). Examples of unsexy problems are even more plentiful, however. New

[1] *Nature*, vol. 238, 28 July 1972, pp. 179–80.

nuclear steam supply systems—of which Britain has four still to be proven in commercial service—are just an embarrassment when the real problems for the electricity supply industry are how to build the things more quickly and cheaply, and how to get from them a higher performance. Similarly in medicine a sophisticated surgical transplantation technology for living organs is just an embarrassment when the real problem is to minimise the amount of disease and road accidents that make suitably youthful 'spare parts' available in the first place.

To be more specific, it is widely agreed—outside the motor industry—that an electric propulsion system rechargeable from the (nuclear) mains overnight must eventually replace our 'frivolous' use of oil by the private car. An electric car should not only conserve oil on an immense scale; it should also free cities from much of the fumes and noise now caused by traffic. The missing technological link is a method of storing electricity with the reliability of the lead-acid battery, but with a power-to-weight ratio about five times as great. Unfortunately electrochemistry—the science of batteries—is a very unsexy subject and intellectually difficult too. Very few first-class scientists have been electrochemists. Yet only through a much more profound understanding of the electrochemistry of batteries—Rothschild himself suggests the problem calls for perhaps fifty man-years of professional effort—can we hope to achieve electric propulsion of adequate utility for the private motorist.

Will Rothschild work?

'The rustic simplicity of agricultural life is a myth that dies hard,' commented Dr. H. C. Pereira, presenting the first report on research and development ever to come from the Ministry of Agriculture, Food and Fisheries (MAFF) in 1973.[1] Agriculture was an industry that already leaned heavily upon science; science which the ministry organised into new farming systems, which in turn gave the industry a growth rate in output per man that was twice that of the manufacturing industries. In two decades, said Pereira, agricultural output had risen from supplying 40 per cent of Britain's needs to 60 per cent. But the pressures this progress imposed accentuated the technical problems remaining, especially problems of disease.

If one puts aside what is spent by private industry on research into farm chemicals and agricultural machinery, agricultural research and development in Britain divides into two big camps. MAFF itself spends about £8–9 million and the Agricultural Research Council

[1] The government's White Paper of 1972 had called upon departments to produce an annual report of their research and development activities.

(ARC) another £22 million (1973–4 figures). Broadly speaking the difference between the two research efforts is that the research council is generating the basic information for the ministry to build into farming systems and techniques.

But for many years, until Rothschild reported, the ministry and the research council were drifting apart. While the farmers' grumbles grew louder that their problems were being neglected, research council and ministry took little interest in each other's policies.

Agricultural research

Pereira, when first offered the post of chief scientist at MAFF, as called for under the reorganisation, rejected the offer. He was director of one of the biggest of the ARC's laboratories, the East Malling Research Station, specialising in the growing of fruit, and he frankly told a Select Committee that he was disturbed by the whole Rothschild plan. (Rothschild had originally proposed that the responsibility for about three-quarters of the ARC budget should be transferred to the ministry's control.) Six months later he learned that, unless he accepted, MAFF was considering appointing an administrator instead of a scientist into this very critical post. Before finally accepting, Pereira asked for a meeting of the directors of all ARC laboratories, to tell them the position and discover whether in accepting the post he could assure himself of their backing.

Pereira is exceptionally well qualified for this diplomatically difficult post. A soil physicist with practical experience in hydrology and land use, he has spent recent years as a scientific administrator for agricultural affairs in central Africa. In Whitehall his first priority was to convince the ARC scientists that MAFF urgently needed their help and had no intention of disrupting their research programme. Above all the ministry would not be interfering with the management of the ARC, despite the fact that by 1976 it would be in control of over half of the ARC funds.[1]

As for any changes in the direction of research, both sides agreed to be guided by a joint consultative organisation—the first real forum the agricultural community had ever had for debating research priorities. This joint consultative organisation was itself to be served by a computer model prepared by the ARC's planning unit, which catalogues details of all agricultural research in Britain. From this model can be drawn pictures of where the effort is going, nationwide, and what it is costing—a facility no other large sector of

[1] The White Paper specified the transfer of £10 million by 1976, but there is nothing to stop MAFF spending more of its own funds on research contracts with the ARC.

British science enjoys. The model has shown clearly that Rothschild's judgment on apples was right—Britain is spending disproportionately heavily on fruit research and neglecting such areas as research on beef cattle.

Pereira places great emphasis on the co-ordination of ARC research with MAFF's experimental activities on stations and farms around the country, where about £2 million of its research funds are spent. He wants to see more experiments carried out on the farms. 'We've got to get together a much more integrated attack on problems—one that includes the managerial ability of the advanced farmer.' The kind of problems which are already yielding to a co-ordinated effort are the eradication of those diseases—brucellosis and mastitis are well-known examples—where the basic research has been successful but the answers are still a long way from being successful in practice.

At the research end, Pereira believes that practically everything in the ARC's research programme is potentially of interest to MAFF. On the other hand, in no sector does he plan to assume complete control. He hopes each ARC institute will share staff time between the pursuit of new ideas and the search for practical solutions to farming problems. An example of a problem of basic research is finding a way of increasing crop yields of legumes (peas, beans, and so on) comparable with the increases in cereal yields of recent years. It is a particularly difficult problem for science to solve because of a stubborn biological link between protein content of the crop and the yield, which causes one to fall as the other is raised. Pereira admits that in the short term at least the best hope of reducing the £100 million a year[1] Britain spends on imported protein for animal food-stuffs lies with the agricultural industry's efforts to make far better use of the proteins in grasses and forage. The manufacture of semi-synthetic (single cell) protein, by such routes as British Petroleum, ICI, Ranks Hovis McDougall and Shell are exploring, offer a small but useful addition to national supplies. There are prospects of obtaining as much as 200,000 tons from this source by 1980—a tenth of the amount we import today. Rapid technical progress is being made to overcome the difficulties of building big continuous fermentation plants for protein. Heavy investment is involved, but in the longer term these plants could make important contributions to Britain's food supplies.

Medical research

Sir Douglas Black, professor of medicine at the University of Manchester, was no happier than Dr. Pereira with the original

[1] Approximate 1971 and 1972 figures.

Rothschild report. (Medical scientists, you will remember, made
most of the fuss, in public at least.) But Black brings both wit and
great charm to his task. Rothschild, he believes, underestimated the
influence that the Department of Health and Social Security (DHSS)
could already exert over the Medical Research Council (MRC). But
the influence was exerted only at top-most level, through Sir George
Godber, until 1973 the government's chief medical adviser. Black's
predecessor as chief scientist, who had come from the MRC, had
wielded no influence whatsoever in that quarter until Rothschild's
report was published. Black, on the other hand, comes to the
job as one of the most highly respected medical scientists in
Britain.

Despite his reservations, Black accepts that Rothschild made two
important points in his report: that government departments (including DHSS) were exerting too little influence on the relevant national
research programmes, and that there was poor liaison between departments with problems and research workers who might have (or
might discover) solutions.

Where Pereira's research budget effectively doubled with the
initial transfer of funds from research council to departmental control, Black's research budget burgeoned from about £1·5 million to
over £10 million. Rothschild's use of the statistics of hospital bed
occupancy as the yardstick to measure the relevance of the MRC's research programme to the sickness of Britons uncovered whole sectors
of sickness—mental illness, the rheumatic diseases, bronchitis—that
the MRC saw as unsexy and largely ignored. Black and his colleagues
admit freely that some of the research they now want to fund in co-
operation with the MRC is 'not of the highest excellence'. An example
would be research to aid the mentally handicapped—spastics, epilep-
tics and the so-called 'lame brains' resulting from injury. 'But if you
argue that it must be of the highest excellence, you won't get anything
started.' Success, they acknowledge, is crucially dependent upon the
ministry's powers to persuade scientists that the work, though unsexy, is well worth doing.

Research to alleviate human sickness cannot be categorised in
quite the same way as research to develop a new process or product.
Rothschild differentiated clearly between basic research (acquisition
of knowledge) and applied research (directed to a goal). In the
medical sector a more subtle distinction would be:

Biomedical research←→clinical research←→health care

Biomedical research is the province of the MRC, and also the pharmaceutical industry (sometimes in collaboration). Health care is the
province of DHSS. Clinical research is an interface of immense concern

to both research council and ministry (and the pharmaceutical industry).

Black approaches the problem of closer liaison between these three sectors with one simple rule: 'In science policy you cannot win.' He has created an elaborate web of high-level committees in an attempt to harmonise relations between the three sectors, and to take account of situations whose problems cross many boundaries in the health and social services sector—for example, the aged, the handicapped, research on nursing methods. His aim is to harmonise relations with the MRC to the point where DHSS is contracting for all its biomedical research from this quarter, while the health care research is being done collaboratively by the two parties.

At this exploratory phase of ministry-MRC negotiations a number of possible customer–contractor relationships are being studied.[1] The independent approach from two sides of the problem initiated by DHSS is illustrated by a project on intensive care treatment of heart attacks. The fact that North America has so enthusiastically endorsed the case for intensive care has led to pressure in Britain to provide more facilities. Yet some of the pressure is founded not on facts but assumptions about the efficacy of treatment. DHSS and MRC are examining independently the special-care and clinical aspects of intensive care, and will pool their findings before the Health Service decides whether to commit large resources.

The significance of mildly or moderately high blood pressure, where there is good evidence that the trouble can be treated before any symptoms of cardio-vascular disease starts to show, has produced a second kind of collaboration. The DHSS wants to be quite sure of the value of the diagnosis, for the consequences in terms of mass-screening and treatment could be very costly. So MRC and DHSS are working in concert, one organising the clinical trials while the other looks after the health care aspects.

A third example of a customer–contractor relationship is a project to compare the various methods for the treatment of rheumatism. It could be argued by the MRC scientists that this would be alleviation, not a basic attack on a disease problem. Nevertheless, DHSS and MRC are now planning a joint research unit for carrying out such an assessment. It could be the forerunner of many such units concerned with the alleviation of distress rather than cures or prevention.

The new relationship is summed up well by Sir John Gray, secretary of the MRC, in his introduction to the council's 1974 annual report: 'The change in the rationale is inevitably away from the extreme "laissez faire" view which holds that the good of society is

[1] David Fishlock, 'Fashion worries for science research', the *Financial Times*, 7 November 1973.

best achieved by the sum of the independent interests of individual
scientists. While the movement is away from laissez faire, however,
the changes at present proposed do not nearly approach that central
direction which has so often been feared as the consequence to be
expected from various recent reports to Government. In broad terms
the situation appears to be one in which it is recognised by all parties
that the ideas and interests of the individual scientists at the bench
are the driving force behind science. If this force is to be used to the
best effect in achieving the practical aims of society, scientists must be
attracted into areas most likely to achieve the desired ends and stimu-
lated to undertake particular investigations; there may also need to be
active discouragement of over-populated but low priority areas . . .'

Industrial research

At the Department of Industry Dr. Ieuan Maddock, as chief scientist,
faces a bigger problem than either Black or Pereira, and a much more
complex situation. His department deals with a very broad sector of
industry and commerce. It concerns itself with the activities of many
of the big research-conscious companies in Britain, and with the
activities of the vastly more numerous medium-size and small companies that earn such a big slice of the nation's wealth. For nearly a
decade now, since Mintech was first created, this sector of government
has been trying to persuade the medium-size and small companies
to make greater use of the scientific resources available in Britain.

It has encouraged its own big research establishments to get out
into industry and make themselves and their expensive facilities and
their considerable skills known. It has encouraged the forty or so
industrial research associations to do the same, in some cases with
generous grants for those who succeeded. It has also encouraged the
independent contract research organisations, by placing contracts
both directly with them, and through its agency, the National
Research Development Corporation. In 1973–4 it spent over half of
its research and development budget of £65 million on contracts with
industry.

Maddock, a physicist in atomic weapons research who joined
Mintech in 1965 to help reorganise its research effort, has been
immensely frustrated by the reluctance of so many companies to
avail themselves of the nation's research and development facilities.
His conclusion is that the basic reason for this reluctance is quite
simply that they lack the technical competence to recognise the value
of what is being offered. Often, because of the multi-disciplinary
nature of so many problems nowadays, they fail to see when they are
getting out of their depth. The research-conscious company recognises

when it lacks data in some crucial sector, and knows that there are two ways of getting that data: from its own research workers or by buying the knowledge from someone else. It can often be quicker and cheaper to go to a contract research organisation with special facilities and experience—it might be a wind-tunnel, a heat-transfer rig or toxicological skills, for example—and purchase the missing data.[1] Maddock also feels very strongly about the distortions introduced by following the dictates of fashion. 'How often do we hear the cry that we must do so and so because everyone else is doing it without critically examining whether it is worth doing anyway or whether it is relevant to the particular company or country?' Avoiding this trap, says Maddock, calls for an interplay—'which may lead to collision' —between the enthusiasts and the uncommitted. 'It was this type of questioning challenge that Lord Rothschild was seeking when he proposed the customer–contractor relationship in government-funded research.'

But as 'customer' in the customer–contractor relationship, Industry is in a less clearly defined situation than, say, DHSS or MAFF or Defence. For example, it has a broad statutory responsibility to work for the 'national good' in such sectors as standards and industrial safety. Who then should decide where its efforts and cash should be directed? What should be the forum for the questioning challenge of the interplay between enthusiast and uncommitted or critic?

Its answer has been to create a 'proxy customer'. Each of its newly-appointed requirements boards represents a body of 'customers' and is charged with responsibility for taking a broad view of their needs in the customer–contractor relationship. Half of them have an industrialist as the chairman. Their purpose, above all, is to increase the relevance of research, whether in-house or under contract, paid for by Industry. Each must fight for the cash it deploys; each must monitor the way it is spent. They must decide whether Industry's performance in selling, say, desalination plant warrants yet more government research funds than the £5 million already spent.

Nine requirements boards have been set up:
1. Computers systems and electronics
2. Ship and marine technology
3. Mechanical engineering and machine tools
4. Chemical and mineral processes and plant
5. Engineering materials
6. Metrology and standards
7. Fundamental standards
8. Aaircraft research
9. Aaviation systems research

[1] Contract Research, *Financial Times* Survey, June 1973.

Except for perhaps 10 per cent of basic research, the laboratories of the Department of Industry are now funded through the requirements boards. Similarly the research associations have become contract research centres working primarily for these boards. If the relevant requirements board refuses to support a proposal, the work must cease unless the laboratory can find a sponsor elsewhere. The national laboratories are free to seek sponsorship overseas but only if they can show that they have exhausted all possibilities of support in Britain.

Already these boards are exerting a powerful influence on research attitudes in government science—by questioning whether the object is a new product, or a process of clear commercial or social value, or is simply a case of curiosity or 'me too'. They should minimise the risks of projects born of euphoria; of another tracked hovercraft, for example, desperately searching for a possible market to justify the very large expense.

Sir Frederick Dainton, in a conversation soon after the White Paper appeared in 1972, compared the damage the more vociferous opponents of Rothschild had done to their own case in the government's eyes, with the damage the more radical students had done a little earlier by some of their actions. The sternest part of the chief scientists' initial task in implementing Rothschild was to rebuild from the wreckage a partnership between science and society of an intimacy that had not existed since the Second World War. Fortunately for both parties, it proved a challenge sufficient to attract some of Britain's best scientific talent. This talent in turn formed its own committee, creating a bond between departments of government that had never existed before. Upon the retirement of Sir Alan Cottrell, the government's chief scientific adviser, in 1974 this committee of departmental chief scientists shouldered the task of advising the Cabinet on science matters.

CHAPTER 11

Anatomy of a tripartite project

'I believe in teams of odd numbers—and sometimes three is too many.'
Torsten Lindstrom, technical director of ASEA, quoted in the *Financial Times* on the management of industrial research, 1974

One November afternoon in 1973 at a meeting in Marlow, a pretty town on the Thames west of London, the appointment was confirmed of Tom Tuohy as new chief executive of the Anglo-German-Dutch uranium enrichment project. Tuohy's immediate task was to turn an audacious experiment in international relations into a large-scale commercial operation based on a novel technology. On the time-scale agreed he had precisely three years to assemble about 100,000 machines and get them running in concert at speeds of upwards of 50,000 r.p.m. And he had competition; not just from the United States as might have been expected but right on his doorstep in Europe for, before the month was out, France had confirmed its intention of pressing ahead with a rival project called Eurodif that would compete for markets in Europe. I propose to discuss this tripartite project at length for it affords important lessons for those seeking successful international collaborations in the exploitation of high technology.

For Tuohy the challenge was the latest in a long association with nuclear production projects, dating back to Britain's first efforts to make fissile materials for its nuclear weapons programme immediately after the Second World War. His experience of intractable problems included one very few men would relish. He was thirty-nine and deputy general manager in charge of production at Britain's atomic factory at Windscale on the day fire broke out in one of the massive plutonium 'piles'. For nearly forty-eight hours he led the battle to conquer the fire that threatened to spread radio-activity over the north-west of England. It was a battle that gives this assertive, Irish-born chemist justification for calling himself, with characteristic bravado, 'the world's most experienced nuclear fire-fighter'.

But at fifty-six Tom Tuohy was taking on perhaps the most difficult task of his career: 'fire brigade' action to ensure the success of the

Anglo-German-Dutch plan to mount a European challenge to a virtual US industrial monopoly already earning over £200 million in 1974 and expected to be earning nearly £3,000 million a year by 1980. Tuohy's talents for turning new technology into large-scale production were talents the project desperately needed at this point in its career.

The project had started two years before, although its origins lay in research work begun separately and secretly by the governments of Britain, the German Federal Republic and the Netherlands more than a decade earlier. In 1971 the three governments had ratified the tripartite treaty of collaboration in exploiting commercially the gas centrifuge method of uranium enrichment. The logic underlying this treaty was that three nations, well-matched in engineering skills, having started their clandestine research efforts from the same basis at the same time, had apparently made very similar progress and reached a very similar conclusion about the technology's future prospects. But the problems of turning the research into a major commercial operation were such that by pooling technology, markets and cash they would stand a much better chance of success.

When in 1968 the idea of a tripartite collaboration was first explored the problems that loomed were almost overwhelming. Each country, believing itself to be ahead of the others, was hinting at its achievements while jealously guarding precise details of progress. In any event all were bound by agreements with the United States which forbade disclosure of details of uranium enrichment technology. Also on the diplomatic front was Germany's particular problem that the world—and especially the Eastern World—would view with alarm any West German plans for large-scale uranium enrichment. For Holland there was another problem. It had no nuclear power programme and hence no domestic market to serve as a base for commercial exploitation. Overshadowing all for the technical experts, however, was the problem of mass-producing a high-performance machine to a very rigid specification on performance and price. Some millions of gas centrifuges would be required to build an enrichment plant with the output of just one of the three huge US plants. And all these machines must be kept running night and day for years at a stretch.

Recognition of this last problem had stopped Britain from pursuing the gas centrifuge route to uranium enrichment to make the explosive for an atomic weapon early in the Second World War. The task would have left few engineering resources for the rest of the war effort.

Enriching uranium

The difficulty in isotope separation or 'enrichment' is that chemical methods of separation are ruled out. Isotopes can be separated only by differences in physical properties. When the isotopes differ by only about one per cent in mass, and when the desired isotope is present to the extent of less than one per cent, as is the case with uranium, the engineering resources required reach astronomical proportions.

Enrichment, in the context of this discussion, is the process of increasing the fissile isotope uranium 235, normally present in natural uranium to the extent of only 0·7 per cent. It makes possible the use of smaller and cheaper nuclear reactors. To put it another way, uranium enrichment is a way of storing energy in a remarkably compact form, readily shipped anywhere in the world, for release later by a nuclear reactor.[1] No more efficient way of storing electrical energy has been discovered.

Only one process for enrichment has been harnessed on a commercially significant scale—that is, thousands of tonnes of 'separative work' a year. It is called gaseous diffusion, a form of ultra-filtration requiring a gaseous form of uranium to be pumped through an endless succession of very fine filters, each of which achieves a tiny 'enrichment' (theoretically 1·004 times) of the desired isotope.

No industrial plant is quite so awesome inside as a gaseous diffusion plant, with its immensely bulky boiler-like units that filter vast volumes of uranium hexafluoride gas, its endless trunking and the dreadful roar of giant compressors. It is elephantine in another respect too; controlling a plant, I was told once, is like steering an elephant—'It reacts so slowly you have time to jump down and give it a kick.' What nowadays is considered an economically competitive scale of gaseous diffusion demands a plant of around 9,000 tonnes of separative work a year. Along with the 2,500MW of power such a factory would need to drive the compressors, the capital outlay today would be upwards of £750 million.

Gaseous diffusion was the enrichment technology that emerged successfully from the crash programme of the wartime Manhattan Project. But twenty-five years before two British scientists, in a theoretical appraisal of isotope enrichment, had written these prophetic words: 'None of the physical methods considered gives hope of easy separation, even for gaseous isotopes. The most promising method appears to be the use of a centrifuge provided the engineering prob-

[1] The industry uses the term 'separative work' to measure the output of an operation from which, despite all the effort expended, the product emerges almost unchanged.

lem can be overcome.'[1] The technique was to tax some of the best technical brains of the post-war generation; men like the late Hans Kronberger who, when a centrifuge burst at Harwell in 1949 causing, as he later described it, 'the laboratory to turn through 90 degrees', was asked by his research director to take the project elsewhere.

Like gaseous diffusion, the centrifuge as an enrichment technique is deceptively simple. When a gaseous mixture of the two isotopes is spun very fast, the heavier molecule tends to move a bit faster towards the wall of the centrifuge rotor. How much faster is crucially dependent upon speed—the efficiency of separation increases as the fourth power of the wall speed of the rotor. Experiments during the 1940s with 'souped-up' modifications of the liquid centrifuges used in the chemical industry showed that the gas centrifuge principle worked, but also highlighted the immense engineering problems, not to mention the dangers from these extremely highly stressed machines 'crashing'—that is, bursing under the centrifugal force, wrecking others and releasing their toxic and highly corrosive contents. By comparison, the elephantine technology of gaseous diffusion was comparatively docile.

Enter Dr. Zippe

Turning point for the gas centrifuge came in 1960 when a German physicist, Dr. Gernot Zippe, who had been working in Russia and later in the United States, published his idea for a light-weight machine that broke right away from the clumsy adaptations of liquid centrifuges. Zippe's machine was supported from the bottom, spinning like a child's top on a simple pin-and-jewel bearing. To stop the rotor from toppling Zippe provided a magnetic bearing at the top. He spun the rotor with a simple but very high speed eddy current motor. His rotor was an aluminium alloy cylinder about twelve inches long and three inches in diameter, enclosed in a high-vacuum chamber—partly to prevent drag when spinning at supersonic speeds and partly to try to contain the debris should the rotor burst under the high centrifugal forces.

In this way Zippe provided a graceful solution for a very intractable problem: the combination of very high centrifuge speeds with a machine simple and reliable enough to be manufactured in very large numbers. How far one could reach in performance—how fast and how long one could make the machine—now depended primarily on the quality of the materials used and the skills with which they were fashioned.

[1] F. A. Lindemann and F. W. Aston, 'The possibility of separating isotopes', *Philosophical Magazine*, vol. 37, no. 6, 1919, p. 523.

Publication of Zippe's ideas[1] excited interest in Britain, Germany and Holland as a 'breakthrough' that conceivably could compete economically with the gaseous diffusion process. The two great attractions for all three nations were first, that with centrifuges one could achieve enrichment with a very much smaller factory than with diffusion. The output would be commensurately small but the process would yield useful levels of enrichment, whereas diffusion demanded an immensely large plant before useful levels of enrichment could be reached. The second great attraction was that the centrifuges, spinning almost friction-free on their pin-and-jewel bearings, would demand far less energy than the great compressors needed to force gas through thousands of ultra-fine filters.

If, therefore, the engineering problems could be solved, the gas centrifuge promised eventually to be a cheaper way of providing the enrichment required by the great majority of nuclear reactors being constructed or contemplated. Enrichment accounts for roughly one-third of the price of nuclear fuel—say about £20,000 a tonne. The machine, moreover, clearly had much more potential for development than gaseous diffusion, a process that had already been researched intensively since the early days of the war. The theoretical enrichment factor per centrifuge was far greater than for gaseous diffusion. The crucial questions for the gas centrifuge were how cheaply could machines be mass-produced and how long would they last.

A 'club' is born

The idea of a tripartite collaboration came about in two clear steps. First, disclosures of progress in Holland early in 1968 alerted the Germans to the possibility of a German-Dutch collaboration in which commercial enrichment plant would be built on Dutch soil, avoiding a diplomatic row with Russia. Then Britain, recognising that the German-Dutch plan could compete with its own aspirations in the enrichment market, proposed a tripartite collaboration.

Britain, with a 400-tonne gaseous diffusion plant at Capenshurst in Cheshire, built originally to provide military enrichment—high-level enrichment for submarine reactor fuel as well as explosives—had been experimenting in parallel with both technologies. In 1967, before news of German and Dutch achievements came to light, the UK Atomic Energy Authority took a secret decision in favour of the centrifuge for future British enrichment capacity. Before the British government would endorse that decision, however, it asked a senior

[1] G. Zippe, *The Development of Short Bowl Centrifuges: Final Report*, USAEC Report ORO.315, 1960.

committee of industrialists to investigate. They confirmed that the right decision had been made by the nuclear scientists. Nevertheless, Dr. Ned Franklin, chief executive of British Nuclear Fuels, one of the key figures in the original decision, admits that those who took it were 'somewhat relieved' when the following year the Dutch and the Germans revealed that they had reached the same conclusion. Further confirmation came early in 1972 when the United States, after several years of strong criticism of the European centrifuge plan,[1] announced its intention of spending heavily on centrifuge technology to see if Europe could be right after all.

Early in 1969 enough details were exchanged between the three prospective European partners to convince all three that they had the technical basis for a well-balanced collaboration. Even so, it took another two years to agree and ratify the Almelo Treaty of Collaboration.

The tripartite treaty agreed to the construction of an initial 350 tonnes of enrichment capacity, to demonstrate on a commercially credible scale the laboratory work of the previous decade. The technology was to be chosen by the three partners from the pool of experience they could now assemble. Meanwhile, the three partners would agree on a research and development programme designed to produce a second-generation centrifuge technology born of the best ideas of all three. This new technology would be needed from about 1976. All new proposals by members for centrifuge research were to be offered first to the tripartite 'club'.

Right from the start, then, it was a central assumption that three mutually respected research efforts, working quite independently, would have resolved key questions of design and manufacture in significantly different ways. If the best ideas could be pooled, the technology should take a major step forward. The clue to this assumption lies in the crucial importance of very long life-times for these machines if the process is to prove economic. Machines must be capable of running non-stop, unattended, for many years. The most trivial changes in materials, design or manufacturing methods must be exhaustively tested. The consequences of an apparently inconsequential change—say in the method of machining the rotor —may not show up until a couple of years of life testing on the complete machine has been achieved and then rotors suddenly begin to burst. An obvious parallel is the role of toxicity testing in pharmaceutical research.

---

[1] Ostensibly on the grounds that it would jeopardise the chances of any international agreement for the non-proliferation of nuclear weapons, but strictly because it threatened the US enrichment monopoly.

Tripartite technology

When the wraps were removed from the technology of the three partners late in the summer of 1971, initial reaction was one of delight that the theoretical basis of the collaboration should have been demonstrated so well. Experts from all three countries were saying the same sort of thing—that ideas neatly complemented each other, especially ideas for mass-producing the gas centrifuge's very few but highly sophisticated components. A new centrifuge born of this pool of ideas seemed quite certain.

For practical purposes there are two distinct kinds of gas centrifuge, differentiated as 'sub-critical' and 'super-critical' machines. Zippe's original centrifuge rotor, as we have seen, was simply a slender cylinder about twelve inches long. The longer this rotor can be made, the greater the output from a machine. But there is a critical speed at which any shaft—and the rotor behaves like a shaft—begins to vibrate elastically, like a violin string. For a rotor of a given stiffness or rigidity, the longer the rotor the lower this first critical speed. It also becomes heavy and Zippe's elegant suspension system can no longer be used.

The skill for the gas centrifuge designer lies in selecting an optimum combination of speed and size (hence complexity), cost and lifespan. Both Germany and Holland had developed super-critical machines. Four German companies (Dornier, MAN, ERNO and Interatom), using government funds, in addition to the government laboratory at Julich, started a centrifuge development during the 1960s. With the introduction of supercritical designs in the late 1960s, the Germans achieved a big increase in centrifuge separative capacity. These new designs began life-testing early in 1971.

In Holland, Zippe's report revitalised disappointing research done during the 1950s, and led to a new government-funded programme led by Professor Martin Bogaart, at the Netherlands Reactor Centre in Amsterdam. By 1967 work on super-critical designs reached the point of assembling a pilot cascade of a couple of hundred machines, completed late in 1968, on which life-testing and cascade testing could be performed simultaneously. By the end of 1972 the Dutch had over 600 machines running in the pilot plant at Almelo in the south of Holland.

In Britain, after post-war work at Harwell, centrifuge studies were started again by the UK Atomic Energy Authority in 1958 in its laboratories at Capenhurst. By 1964–5 a team led by Mr. Jack Parry had a sub-critical machine, simple but of high separation capacity, and believed suitable as the basic unit of an economic centrifuge plant. The first of these machines was put on life-test in 1966. By the time the three partners began pooling their data in 1971, Britain could claim uninterrupted runs of over five years on individual machines, and the successful commissioning earlier that year of a pilot cascade of over 200 machines. One very significant feature of this cascade was how tightly the centrifuges were packed, like living cells, demonstrating a very high level of confidence in this highly rated machine. Less confidence means that machines must be spaced further apart and more elaborate safeguards must be taken to prevent the kind of accident that occurred at Oak Ridge, usa, in 1973, when a crash destroyed part of an experimental centrifuge enrichment plant.

Before the tripartite treaty had been ratified, all three nations had begun independently to assemble three small centrifuge enrichment plants, of similar size, totalling about 90 tonnes capacity. The British plant was at Capenhurst, adjoining the diffusion plant; the Dutch and German plants were at Almelo. All were seen as demonstration plants, aimed at amassing detailed information on the mass-production of machines and the operation of centrifuge cascades. The British and Dutch plants came into operation late in 1972, and the German plant about six months later. Between them they represented five different centrifuge concepts, and three different ways of arranging them to form an enrichment plant.

Tripartite companies

These three pilot plants were acquired later by Urenco, commercial arm of the organisation set up under the tripartite treaty to develop and exploit the three centrifuge technologies. This organisation and its shareholders is shown in *figure 11*. Urenco, based in Marlow, would own the centrifuge enrichment plants and market their product. Another tri-national company called Centec, based in Bensberg near Cologne, would take responsibility for the design and construction of centrifuge plants, including the assembly of the machines and the research and development programme to keep the technology advancing. They began as very small organisations, just a few dozen people apiece, but each was backed up by three industrial shareholding organisations representing the one-third interest of each of the partners.

So closely were Centec and Urenco to work together, however, that within two years it became clear that a more unified management structure was needed. The companies shared the same central problem—assembly and installation of machines in sufficiently large numbers, to exacting standards of performance and cost. 'Watch-making at alarm-clock prices,' as one scientist described it to me.[1] By

[1] A Dutch centrifuge engineer has told me that the cost of making the early lightweight centrifuges worked out at about £20,000 apiece.

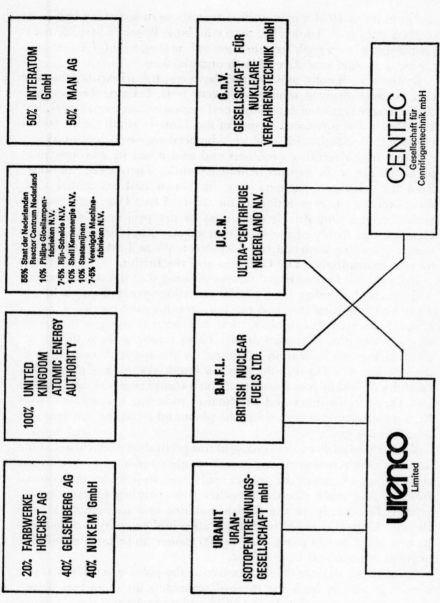

Figure 11 Relationships between the two tripartite companies, Urenco and Centec, and their shareholders.

the autumn of 1973 a new unified management structure had been worked out. Tom Tuohy, the man who built Britain's first 25-tonne centrifuge plant, replaced the general managers of Centec and Urenco, as chief executive of both organisations.

By the time Tuohy took charge, however, the tripartite structure had already survived some very severe tests. Britain, for example, had a longer record of centrifuge performance than its partners, but based on a less advanced design of machine, of small development potential. Holland, with a more advanced super-critical machine, ran into manufacturing problems and as a result its 25-tonne pilot plant fell about six months behind schedule. There were rumblings from the other two partners that the Dutch had overstated their claims during the negotiations of the treaty. I recall one conversation with German and British executives of the project in which the German was firmly of the view that success would depend on one nation assuming leadership of the project. When I asked which one, he said disarmingly, 'The Germans and the British.'

By late 1972 Centec issued figures showing that the three partners had amassed running time of 550 centrifuge-years between them. They had machines that had run non-stop for over six years, and a cascade (about 200 machines) that had been running non-stop for nineteen months. Autopsies on machines removed from these tests were giving no indication of limits on life-span. A consensus of opinion was forming that the first few hundred tonnes of production capacity should be based essentially on a combination of the German and Dutch centrifuges and production techniques, combined with British experience of organising the plant and handling the uranium hexafluoride gas.

Two events early in 1973 changed this preliminary conclusion. One was stiff new terms proposed by the US government for enrichment supplies, which meant the project could raise its price for enrichment from its first small plant. The other was currency changes which reacted favourably on the British machine and its manufacture in Britain. Urenco decided to increase its initial capacity and to order its first plant in two parts, each of 200 tonnes, to be built simultaneously at Almelo and Capenhurst.

Tuohy took over as chief executive at the point when Urenco was receiving tenders from the three shareholders for these two plants. The outcome was a decision to build a plant at Almelo based essentially on a German design of machine with Dutch refinements, assembled in factories in Germany; and a plant at Capenhurst based on a British design of machine, assembled in a factory on the Capenhurst site. These plants were to be completed by the end of 1976, at a cost of about £40 million. They would require the assembly, test and installation of a total of about 100,000–200,000 gas centrifuges. The cost of the machines alone would work out at about £20 million —about £100 apiece.

Tripartite research project

Apart from sharing the cost and the risk, an important part of the logic of collaboration, it will be recalled, was the idea that by pooling design and manufacturing data, the three partners should quickly develop a common second-generation technology, combining the best ideas of the three. On the time-scale dictated by the urgent need to break into the commercial enrichment market, in competition with plans for greatly extended capacity for gaseous diffusion, it was not possible to consider pooled technology for the first production plants. Life-testing alone would have taken at least two years; without this information there can be no confidence in estimates of plant costs. The treaty called, however, for a common research and development programme, to develop the technology that would be needed from the mid-1970s. Urenco later announced that during the period 1976–80 it expected its centrifuge capacity to grow from 400 to about 2,000 tonnes. By 1974 the company had signed contracts absorbing almost all the capacity anticipated by 1980.

An integrated research, development and life testing[1] programme has been worked out by the two companies. The three 'club' members had chosen different ratios of speed and rotor length to achieve their objectives. The 'club' decided which paths offered the greatest development potential and what research should be stopped. No new laboratories were set up, but the 'club' allocated some £10 million for the first year (1973) of a joint research programme spanning about ten research centres in the three countries; not the optimum way, admits Jack Parry, technical manager of Urenco, who has charge of one part of the programme, but certainly the way to get a programme launched quickly and to make fullest use of the facilities that exist.

One obvious risk—albeit one that might not come to light for some years—is that the country whose research centre is working on the key components could get the inside track for big industrial contracts. The key components are the rotor and its suspension which between them account for about 25 per cent of the cost of a centrifuge plant.

The joint research programme is in two parts. One, managed by Parry, aims to develop further the two types of machine now being

---

[1] Life-testing of machines and components is a major part of any centrifuge research programme, accounting for perhaps one-third of its cost.

F

installed: the sub-critical type at Capenhurst where stronger, stiffer materials could increase speed and hence output; and the super-critical type where output can be improved by increasing rotor length as well as speed. The emphasis inevitably is on life-testing. The second part of the programme, under Ir. F. H. Theyse, technical manager of Centec, aims to develop a tripartite technology, more advanced than the technology now being installed. The basic objectives remain the same, however, namely to see how far rotor speed and length can be stretched without undue sacrifice in lifetime and cost. Stronger, stiffer materials such as carbon fibre show great promise here—the centrifuge problem has many features in common with the carbon-fibre fan blades Rolls-Royce tried to use (chapter 3). Whereas aluminium rotors can achieve about 50,000 r.p.m. and steel rotors around 60,000 r.p.m., carbon fibre rotors may reach 100,000 r.p.m. But the cost of carbon-fibre must fall by a factor of ten or greater before the centrifuge club will be ready to take advantage of this method of making light but stiff rotors.

Lessons learned

'The capacity of enrichment plant which Urenco can provide by 1980 is not going to be determined by technology,' Dr. Ned Franklin confidently announced to UNIPEDE[1] members at a meeting in London in midsummer 1973. Franklin, a rather shy fellow, not given to making extravagant claims, was answering critics who charged that the centrifuge route to enrichment was 'unproved'; too great a risk for Europe to rely heavily upon for the early 1980s. What would determine centrifuge enrichment capacity by 1980, said Franklin, was no longer technology but 'our ability to borrow money to build the plants'. The kind of money he was talking about was upwards of £50 million for each 1,000 tonnes of enrichment capacity. That ability to borrow would in turn be determined by the number of contracts forthcoming from UNIPEDE members and others.

Six crucial lessons, I believe, emerge from the experience of the tripartite 'club' that allowed Franklin to make such a confident assertion to prospective customers after less than two years of collaboration:

1. The importance of the central assumption that knowledge and experience of the subject was well balanced between the 'club' members.
2. The importance of keeping the number of collaborators small.
3. The importance of having a common language.

[1] International Union of Producers and Distributors of Electrical Energy.

4. The importance of having a well-defined market and clear objectives.
5. The importance of having a powerful incentive to meet the objectives—the promises on delivery and price.
6. The importance of having a technology flexible enough to accommodate progress without a major hiccup in output.

I propose to expand these six points a little. First, the central assumption that all partners in a collaboration were equal in knowledge and experience has usually been missing from actual or proposed international collaborations of this kind, particularly in the nuclear and aircraft industries, where the economic advantages of joint ventures seemed greatest. The weaker partners technically inevitably see the partnership as a great opportunity to catch up. If their own contribution happens to be a superior talent for project management, it simply means they will catch up a lot quicker. Theo van den Bergh, the Shell executive who became general manager of Urenco until his retirement in 1973 when Tuohy took over, points to the fact that in those two years Urenco's staff completely lost their habit of thinking nationally about centrifuge technology. They spoke only of tripartite options. Once that point was reached vital decisions became much simpler to take, for chauvinism was no longer confusing the issue.

The second point, keeping the number of partners small, is crucial because the difficulty of taking major decisions in such situations seems to grow not proportionally but as the square of the number of 'club' members. As it was the tripartite project had four instead of three shareholders, for the Germans wanted different industrial consortia to be their shareholders in the two tripartite companies, Centec and Urenco.[1] Initially the centrifuge project ruthlessly excluded Italy and Belgium—to their intense annoyance—despite claims by both to have some experience of centrifuge technology and a home market for enrichment. The decision pushed both nations closer to the French and involvement with the rival Eurodif project. But it was a risk the 'club' had to take in its formative stages, until the major commitments had been made. In 1973, however, the partnership spawned a second 'club', known as ACE, with the idea of exploring joint ventures between Urenco, as marketing arm of the tripartite organisation, and fourth parties (public or private organisations) who might independently exploit Centec's centrifuge technology.

A common working language, point three, came about simply

[1] Pressure from the two groups of German shareholders for a bigger say in investment decisions led to a more decentralised management structure late in 1974, and to Tuohy's resignation.

because the Dutch and the Germans were able and willing to use English.

Point four, a clearly defined market, is another factor missing from many proposals for high-technology projects, as earlier chapters have so often shown. The product in this case is highly specific, enrichment of uranium to specified levels, usually 2–4 per cent. The customers are the electrical utilities of the world, who have alternative sources of supply but no alternative to enrichment as an ingredient of nuclear fuel. The terms are dictated by the competition, for the United States has a virtual monopoly of supplies for some years until the early 1980s. *How* the enrichment is done, however, is of no real concern to the customer provided he can rely on delivery of the purchased amount of 'separative work'.

Point five, the value of having a powerful incentive to meet promises on delivery and price—in short, an urgent need to succeed —is a factor too often waived once a project has been launched. Too often, in the civil as well as the military sector, technical progress— whether initiated by contractor or customer—is allowed to take precedence over the date of completion, with disastrous consequences upon costs. In enrichment, however, the urgency of the need to provide Europe with independence in energy supplies has increased appreciably during the brief life-span of the project, owing to the intransigence of the oil-producing nations.

The sixth and final point, on the flexibility of the technology, is a more subtle one. The gas centrifuge is competing with an established enrichment technology, gaseous diffusion, in which the United States has already invested $2,000 million and plans to spend at least another $1,000 million in expanding existing capacity. But gaseous diffusion is a highly inflexible technology. Once a commitment is made to build plant offering maximum economies of scale, the technology must be frozen—even though there will be no enrichment available for another six or seven years. Any changes will surely delay completion and send plant costs soaring. With the centrifuge, the economies of scale are achieved on the assembly lines rather than in the enrichment plant. Since a handful of machines will deliver the desired levels of enrichment, their installation can be matched very closely to the size of the market. What is more, as bigger, faster designs are proven on the test stands they can be manufactured and put to service without further delay.

It can, I know, be argued that the gas centrifuge is a unique solution to a unique problem. Equally well, I believe, it can be argued that the tripartite gas centrifuge project is unique only because no one else has yet tried to implement these five lessons.

CHAPTER 12

Specification for success

'You can't cure a problem by trampling it to death.'

Dr. Ieuan Maddock, 1973

In a remarkably candid address to the Royal Society in 1968 Dr. Alastair Pilkington, technical director (now chairman) of Pilkington Brothers, told how his company had striven to develop a process used today by every major flat glass manufacturer in the world. By 1973 the float glass process was earning £55 million a year in glass sales for the company and another £13 million in royalties from its licensees.

The bright idea that Pilkington had in 1952 cost the company seven years of research and development effort and £3 million to reach the stage of saleable glass, and then another £4 million in development costs before it supplanted the traditional product, plate glass. For fourteen long months in the late 1950s the process was making unsaleable glass. 'I had to report regularly to the board, and every month put in a requisition to justify another month's expenditure of £100,000.' Fortunately the board's nerve held strong.

The bright idea—seized upon with such enthusiasm that within weeks the scientists had begun to design a £25,000 pilot glassmaking plant—was that glass of a quality competitive with plate glass, which had to be expensively ground and polished, might be made simply by casting glass on to molten metal. The denser metal, if sufficiently still, pure and unreactive, would support a thin ribbon of glass, allowing the forces of gravity and surface tension to make the ribbon perfectly flat. If it worked it would combine the natural brilliance and high production rates of 'fire polished' sheet glass with the optical perfection of mechanically polished plate glass. The market was windows of every description—for homes, shops, office buildings, factories and cars.

'There is a saying,' says Pilkington, 'that the price of progress is trouble.' He left no doubt that some of the troubles thrown up by float glass brought the company close to abandoning the venture. Right from the start there was trouble, even under experimental conditions, in keeping the metal, molten tin, from picking up traces of oxygen, which by forming a skin of oxide marred the mirror finish of the underside of the floating glass. To be a good development man, Pilkington believes, you must be a born optimist. 'That may have been all right for those of us in the development team, but the board were only interested in a cold-blooded, objective analysis of the project and its progress so I had to be both optimistic and objective.'

This combination—so rare, as earlier chapters have shown—proved persuasive this time, for in 1954 the Pilkington board decided to give the float glass project the highest possible priority, in order to decide as soon as it could whether the project was destined for success. Neither could they turn elsewhere for help with most of the many problems that loomed, partly because they themselves were already beyond the boundaries of existing glassmaking science, but also because the commercial implications were so great as to call for tight security. Nonetheless, some of the more sophisticated chemistry was commissioned elsewhere.

'The critical moment—and this was the most important decision that we made in the whole project—came when we decided to step up from the experimental stage to the construction and operation of a full-scale production plant.' When this decision was taken the scientists were still experimenting.

> We thought we were very much more knowledgeable than we turned out to be, when in 1957 we tried to make a competitive, saleable product. Once having set up a production plant, the consequences of failure could have been enormous, and in retrospect we were woefully unaware of the magnitude of the problems we were going to face when we reached a mass production scale. It was a terrific fight to turn the experiment into commercial success.

The first full-scale float glass plant began making glass in May 1957. Not until July 1958 did it make glass that was saleable. Early the following year the company announced to the world its new glassmaking process—in the words of Lord Pilkington, then its chairman, 'the most fundamental, revolutionary and important of all the advances in glassmaking of the present century.'[1] Cheerfully the development team shut down the plant for some long overdue renovations. 'Imagine our disappointment,' said Dr. Pilkington, 'when we started up again and made unsaleable glass.'

Pilkington led his audience along a fascinating trail to show how much science—and how much luck too—lay behind the announcement of success, and even then how much remained to be done. One astonishing piece of good fortune was the discovery early on that no

[1] The *Financial Times*, 21 January 1959.

matter what thickness of glass was delivered on to the molten tin, it always spread out into a film approximately 7 mm thick. Half the company's market for polished plate glass was for glass of this thickness. But, by the same token, it proved very difficult—another two years of 'night and day slog'—to learn how to vary the thickness and thus accommodate the other half of the market. First they had to discover the theoretical basis for such consistency and the magnitude of the forces at work, before they could find ways of gently modifying those forces without introducing distortions.

A problem of a very different kind from the complex chemistry of metal–glass interactions or the physics of floating films of molten glass emerged in anticipating the scale of operations that would open up if the process succeeded. The whole point of the exercise was the continuous, high-volume production of top-quality glass. It called for fully-mechanised handling and storage, with computers responding to customers' orders and instructing the cutting to minimise wastage of glass. Quite apart from float glass, this part of the operation was a major advance in glass technology in its own right.

Lessons from float glass

Sir Alastair Pilkington's[1] story illuminates admirably several very important factors required for commercial success in high-technology ventures. First, it illustrates the magnitude of the scientific effort that may be required to turn a bright idea into a commercial success. The figures, it should be remembered, relate to the 1950s when research costs were very much lower. But down through the 1960s when float glass was in full-scale production the company continued to spend similar sums on research and development to keep the new technology advancing. There was always the risk that one of the company's own licensees would leapfrog with its own developments.

Second, the float glass story demonstrates the importance of taking account from the outset of the consequences of success, in this case the fact that a whole new technology would have to be developed and financed to handle efficiently the tremendous output of high-grade glass sheet. Neglect of this count could have greatly embarrassed the company, even destroyed prospects for the process itself.

Third, it illustrates the importance of having all-party backing once the project has reached the point of serious consideration. The decision of the Pilkington board to go all out to make or break the project ensured that it had their undivided attention, and the scientists had every incentive to make it succeed.

A fourth point that emerges is the importance of high qualities of

[1] Dr. Pilkington was knighted in 1971.

leadership if a project is to surmount not just technical problems—
forbidding as they may seem in the high technology sector—but the
commercial, financial and perhaps social (human relations) problems created by a major technical advance. It is a point brought out
clearly by the findings of the Sappho study, which will be discussed
later. But Pilkington also stresses the need to differentiate between
the directing of a project and the managing of a project—with direction in the hands of someone very senior in the company. 'If the person who is managing it is also asked to direct it, I believe he will fail
to do either job adequately and will find it extremely difficult to
keep the project in perspective.'

A fifth point is the need to identify the key decisions in the life of
the project. For example, the changeover from an experimental project to a production plant is extremely important.

Finally, the Pilkington story illustrates how important it may be
for those taking decision to keep their nerve when, as Kipling puts
it, 'all about you are losing theirs and blaming it on you'. For
the entire Pilkington board, not just the technical director, those
fourteen months when the company was spending £100,000 a
month making glass it could not sell required exceptionally strong
nerves.

Code of the scientist

Unfortunately, the code by which a scientist works disciplines him
to present his discoveries and achievements with a maximum
economy of words. His published papers and presentations are normally stripped of the frustrations and false trails, the mistakes and
misunderstandings, the omissions and the oversights. No experienced
scientist is every fooled by the picture portrayed of a logical progres-
sion from idea or hypothesis to the proof; but neither is he helped
very much by the printed record.

What can fool the scientist who fancies his chances as an entrepreneur, however, is the absence of the same kind of revealing detail
from most of the papers and presentations of those who have turned
science into successful business operations. They, too, normally omit
the frustrations, false trails, mistakes and omissions. They may claim
that they had a prototype running or samples for testing inside a
couple of years, but will neglect to add that it would be five years or
ten years before the company could expect to see a profitable return
on its investment; that they spent much more on other prototypes
that would not work. Still worse, they may well imply that, having
solved all the difficult problems, they are ready now to turn the
prototype over to others and get on with exploring the latest idea. As a

result, a mythology envelops the achievement that can be not just unhelpful but very misleading.

A scientist who for the past decade has been following closely the rise and fall of hundreds of science-based companies around Britain and their competitors overseas is Dr. Ieuan Maddock, chief scientist at the Department of Industry. Dr. Maddock spells out bluntly what is so different about the science-based company—for, make no mistake, it is different in one vital respect from those making bicycles or butter. 'There is no natural end point or plateau in the development of the science-based industries. . . . Generally, there is no point at which we can stop and say "We have gone far enough" and assume that we have reached a long and stable regime in the technology.' This is so no less for the major advance in a traditional industry, such as float glass, than in the aircraft, atomic or electronics industries.[1]

For the scientist with an urge to strike out on his own the question Maddock has attempted to answer is 'Can he survive when the trend so remorselessly is "winner takes all"?'. Research and development costs, frightening though they can be for these industries, are just a small part of the cost of bringing a highly technological product to the market place. Dr. Maddock quotes a us government study published in 1967 on the relative costs of the stages between the bright idea and the market. If research and development leading to the basic invention costs one unit, engineering and product design will absorb another two units, and production capacity and tooling will cost a further seven units. Even then it will cost another three units to get the production flowing.[2] If, after this daunting escalation in outlay, the company still retains the confidence of its bankers, the commercial success of the product will carry it on to still bigger demands for cash. Large manufacturing plant and expensive marketing arrangements will have to be created. The pattern is illustrated in *figure 7*. 'It is safe to say,' counsels Maddock, 'that it will be appreciably more than the cost of bringing the product to the market initially.'

For big companies such as Rolls-Royce no less than the small team of entrepreneurs this can raise a serious question of credibility with its customers. The reason is this: if the company slips just a little in its schedule—and the chances are high that it will—and arrives in the market place behind a more powerful competitor, though in price and performance it may stand up well, it nonetheless is a new arrival. It is challenging an established product, already supported

---

[1] David Fishlock, 'A good invention is not enough', the *Financial Times*, 14 September 1973. (See also *New Scientist*, 6 and 13 September 1973.)
[2] *Technological Innovation: Its Environment and Management*, us Department of Commerce, Washington DC, 1967.

by after-sales service, training schemes, software that makes it more adaptable, and so on.

It is a situation that will stretch the loyalty of the most devoted customer, says Maddock. What if the company's delivery is later than promised? Or the product's performance falls short of the mark? What if, in its efforts to remain in the race, the company over-reaches and goes bust? 'This kind of credibility argument is deep-rooted and very difficult to combat. Only courageous decisions by powerful customers can reverse the trend.'

But this raises a new risk for the entrepreneurs—that he becomes so indebted to powerful friends that they dictate the way he runs his affairs. More and more, he discovers, his company is not so much an entrepreneurial organisation as an operating wing of its main customer.

Lest all this sounds as though Maddock is doing his best to discourage the scientist from venturing into business on his own account, let me say that this is indeed the case. And yet he believes strongly that what Europe needs is far more of these science-based industries. European industry lacks the willingness to rely on specialist sub-contractors of this kind for precision mechanical and electro-mechanical engineering, instrumentation, computers, optical and semi-conductor devices, and all the vast array of increasingly cunning sub-systems that go into complex modern systems—aircraft, power stations, weapons systems, industrial plant. Science-based companies survive and prosper in the United States, he suggests, because they act as highly specialised sub-contractors to a number of competing big-systems companies. They afford a highly sophisticated infrastructure which is important for industrial vitality.

Code of survival

This argument, therefore, leads Maddock to define the characteristics required of a science-based company if it is to have any real hope of survival. He offers the twelve-point specification set out in *table 9* for the kind of company that might survive present pressures. The code, he admits, is somewhat daunting but 'it is right that it should be so'. It leads him to draw three important conclusions.

Maddock's first conclusion, on the growing importance of the customer's role in this sector of commerce, is that ever more powerful manufacturing groups are not enough—the customers themselves must get together and form an industrial base strong enough to give the science-based sub-contractors the all-important opportunity of demonstrating credibility in their products. At the same time, the customer must appreciate the power he wields and be realistic about prices and price escalation.

Table 9 Code of Survival for Science-based Companies

- Must expand resources and skills fast enough to match technological advance.
- Potential sales sufficiently large to keep down fixed research and development costs.
- Must supply 'non-technological' customer inducements—leasing, training, trade-in, spares and maintenance.
- Multi-disciplined enough to exploit new technologies.
- Have powerful customers to place initial orders and show that the product works.
- Have outside suppliers for essential specialist goods and services.
- Strong in a market sector where at no competitive disadvantage.
- Realistic about cost escalation in making forecasts.
- Able to market the product quickly.
- Able to resist temptation to diversify.
- Willing to learn from other innovators.
- Willing to withdraw quickly from disappointing projects.

His second conclusion is that the successful big-system company has to be prepared to adapt by changing its structure so as to accept the services of specialist sub-contractors more readily, and to choose markets better suited to its resources.

Maddock's third conclusion is that the only credible way ahead, offering 'the appropriate level of turnover, while retaining a measure of competition and permitting specialisation coupled with viable operations' is to base advanced technologies on a European-scale rather than a national-scale economy. And here, he warns, time is not on our side.

Project Sappho

In the late 1960s Professor Christopher Freeman, who heads the Science Policy Research Unit at the University of Sussex, had the bright idea of studying closely similar pairs of inventions where the main difference was that one had proved a commercial success and the other a flop. Such a study, he thought, might uncover common ingredients of success or failure for high technology industries—the factors present in the success stories and absent from the flops. Many had before him studied success in trying to find some magic formula that would guarantee it. Freeman recognised that it could be no less valuable to locate the common factors of failure.

He set three researchers to work isolating pairs of innovations as closely matched as they could manage in every respect except one. One had to be a commercial success and the other less so, if not actually a flop. Of about one hundred companies approached in chemicals and scientific instruments, only three refused point-blank to talk. They ended by analysing forty-three pairs of innovations. It called for an exhaustive technique of questioning and the 'recycling' of answers to strip away the mythology which, as we have seen, tends to envelop every innovation. Although float glass—a manufacturing process rather than a novel product—was not among them, the reader cannot fail to see how closely the common characteristics of success are adhered to in the float glass story.

Project Sappho[1] succeeded in isolating several features common to success among the innovations of these two industries. First, the successful companies devoted the greater effort to selling. Second, they made greater attempts to educate the customer. Third, they understood better what the customer wanted. It was clear too—'and we were a bit surprised at this' admitted one of the researchers—that the more successful innovators had stronger links with the scientific and technical community, not necessarily in general but in the specific area concerned.

Behind successful innovation, suggests Sappho, stands a man the researchers call the business innovator. The more successful of each pair of innovations was piloted into the market by a man with more power, more responsibility, and more diverse experience—often including experience abroad—than his opposite number in the firm that failed. Although not necessarily the managing director—he might be a department head or in charge of research and development—the man behind a success was invariably a fairly senior executive, in chemicals in his fifties but in instruments younger, still under forty. He was the man given over-all responsibility for the project and also the link with the world beyond—with science, technology and the market place.

The successful innovator in chemicals turns out to have more responsibility, more power, more diverse experience and a longer record with the company concerned than his competitor. The distinguishing marks of success in instruments turn out to be a greater commitment, greater enthusiasm and greater involvement.

These points come out strongly in the case of a pair of inventions that were particularly well matched: two automatic document readers, the Scandex machine from the Farrington Corporation in

[1] The name Sappho began as a joke on the idea of identical pairings, but was later rationalised as the acronym for 'scientific activity predictor from patterns with heuristic origins'.

the United States and the Solartron machine developed in Britain. Even the customers for these machines matched beautifully—a pair of football pool companies, Vernon's and Littlewood's, wanting them as coupon readers, and a pair of multiple tailors, Montague Burton and John Collier, wanting them to read accounts. Behind Scandex a business innovator (called David Shephard) could be clearly discerned, but this was not so in the case of Solartron, which in 1963 abandoned the chase.

One US chemical project could have fallen flat on its face when at the critical moment the competition slashed the price of its product. But in this case the business innovator had the right combination of marketing and technical experience—and also the nerve—to state flatly that he would undercut the new price.

Float glass, of course, has no pair with which it could be compared and contrasted. But a project with many aspects in common, insofar as it promised to revolutionise another sector of manufacturing technology, the engineering machine shop, was Molins' System 24. The concept of Theo Williamson, Molins' research director until 1973, its aim was to accelerate the manufacture of precision engineering parts by a very big factor, by the application of new metal-cutting technology and by placing the entire process of cutting and handling components under the control of a computer. Unfortunately Molins, after spending very heavily for several years in the 1960s to develop Williamson's concept, lost its nerve when delays and cost escalation threatened to double the cost of the installation the company was making in Bermondsey. In 1970 it abandoned unfinished what should have been the world's first fully automatic machine shop. In 1973 it abandoned the subsidiary set up to sell the System 24 concept and its component machines. Unlike float glass, the technology was at the most a useful adjunct to the parent company's main stream of business, the manufacture of cigarette-making machines.

Why Jewkes goes awry

Early in this book I quoted criticism made by Professor John Jewkes, the Oxford economist, who in his widely publicised Wincott Lecture in 1972 had been so scathing about the achievements of high technology, especially when government got involved in the venture. He placed the blame squarely on government, arguing that British governments in recent years had not been performing their primary tasks 'as successfully as they used to perform them'. Those primary tasks were the obligations 'without success in which all else must come to frustration': defence, maintenance of law and order and justice, maintenance of central standards of measurement including money; prevention of fraud and misrepresentation. It may be, he conceded, that such tasks had become more complicated, less tractable than in the past. But should not a government that found itself unable to cope with its primary tasks shed some of its less important commitments? Involvement in civil high technology was surely one of the first it could drop? It should retain only those involvements with science—university research and government laboratories concerned with public health, safety and well-being—performing services 'which would not otherwise be carried out because a market price cannot be charged for them in the normal way'.

Appealing though this argument is for any taxpayer except possibly a few tens of thousands of scientists and engineers, it displays a confidence in private enterprise that is almost breath-taking, and certainly not warranted on past performance, in Britain or anywhere else. Business, big or small, has no exemplary record of management in the high technology sector. There are only too many miscalculations and clangers to offset such commercial triumphs as Pilkington's float glass process, ici's herbicide paraquat and heart drugs, Beecham's semi-synthetic penicillins, Fison's anti-asthmatic drug Intal, Alfred Herbert's Batchmatics, and other glamour products of the stock market. Far too often companies make the wrong choice, lose their nerve at the critical moment, misread or mistime the market, or—in the immortal words to emerge from the Rolls-Royce bankruptcy inquiry—simply fail to appreciate it was going to cost so much. Expensive miscalculations recently in the private sector, in addition to Rolls-Royce's RB.211 aero-engine, include Courtauld's safer cigarette plans, ici's artificial wool, Hawker Siddeley's Kestrel locomotive, Westland's hovercraft, Molins' System 24, Autonomics' computer software services.

What the argument fails to acknowledge is just how broadly the government of a highly industrialised state must be prepared to interpret the role of defence today. Such a country is vulnerable to interference nowadays in many more ways than by physical assault on its people. The destruction of three jet airliners on an airfield over 2,000 miles away in Jordan in 1970 brought it home finally to the British government—and perhaps many more—just how vulnerable it was to dissident people who saw themselves as having absolutely nothing to lose. At the other end of the spectrum, there are nations so richly endowed with natural resources that no matter how minuscule their population or fighting abilities, they are in a powerful position to influence the policies and prosperity of such nations as Britain. High technology may not have all the answers but is an option no government can afford to close.

Events moved rapidly during 1973 to overtake the Jewkes case for less government involvement in high technology. The major oil companies, high among the more research-conscious organisations in the private sector and already in most cases turning themselves into energy companies with much wider interests than oil, began asking for government help both in oil negotiations with the Oil Producing and Exporting Countries (OPEC) and in the development and exploitation of alternative energy resources. Both public and private sectors recognised they must act quickly and in concert to isolate the weak points and missing data in the current energy scene. For Britain it was all too readily apparent that the weaknesses lay right in the private sector—in the manufacture of materials and components for nuclear and other generating stations, off-shore oil production platforms and pipelines, automatic coalmining equipment and other highly stressed machinery and structures. The need was to refocus research and development effort on these points of weakness without jeopardising longer-range goals of high technology, from sophisticated methods of sea-bed engineering immune from the weather to the exploitation of the fast 'breeder' reactor.

Ten rules for success

I have no 'formula' for success in high technology, any more than my Press colleagues who tip horses have a magic formula for success. If we had we should be far too busy using it to write newspaper advice for the punter in either sector. But even if I thought I had a formula for success I should be very humble indeed in the face of the accumulated wisdom of the National Research Development Corporation, an agency which in 1974 celebrates twenty-five years of experience in supporting high technology in Britain. In a conversation early in 1974 the retiring chief executive, Dr. Basil Bard, summarised its performance in backing R & D ventures: one in three was a write-off, one in three broke even, one in three made some money (see chapter 2). Even so there are those who would say such a record shows that the Corporation is being far too unadventurous—that it should be taking much bigger risks with the taxpayers' money in the larger interests of British invention and innovation.

What, as a writer and commentator on research and technology management, I can try to do for my readers is to distil the lessons brought out in this book. After many re-distillations I have reduced the wisdom to just ten suggestions: five do's and five dont's for those who would indulge in high technology.

1. *Don't be over-ambitious*—the unwritten rules of engineering design and manufacture may be much more crucial to success than the

laws of physics. Sir Sydney Camm, for forty-one years chief designer of Hawkers, had a rule: 'Don't go too far beyond the existing states of knowledge in too many sectors at once.' All too often the way advocated out of existing difficulties takes the venture still deeper into uncharted areas of knowledge.

2. *Don't underestimate lead time*—it can be dauntingly long before a positive cash flow begins, and ten or fifteen years before a new venture in some sectors of high technology begins to yield maximum profits. Everything tends to take longer and cost more than the enthusiast thinks. As Coombs puts it (chapter 6), almost everything unexpected that happens to a development project is bad. Invariably it means delay, greater cost, more risk of missing the market.

3. *Don't set up ventures in isolation from the market*—it will probably make the market even more determined to reject your ideas. The hovertrain, rejected from the outset by British Rail, and the steam-generating heavy water reactor, rejected from the outset by the Central Electricity Generating Board, are expensive examples from recent British experience.

4. *Don't let research and industry drift apart*—the field of British innovation is strewn with the bones of bright ideas that failed to surmount the hurdles of construction and manufacture. The research and design teams that developed new steam turbines for the *Queen Elizabeth II* liner had been allowed to disperse before the wretched maiden voyage in 1970, and had to be hastily re-assembled to rectify the problems of a highly destructive vibration. But the most damaging example in Britain is the gulf that has opened between the UK Atomic Energy Authority and the nuclear design and construction industry. Don't let your scientists remain aloof from the problems of the shop-floor or the construction site. But the corollary of this rule is:

5. *Don't underestimate the scientific mind*—it will not have the answers to every problem but, with encouragement, it can produce far more answers than is usually asked of it. As Waddington has written,[1] treat science as 'a mere speciality to be called in on technical details, then the best [you] can hope for is help on details—and that at a level of originality which one can expect from a man willing to be treated as not competent to contribute to wider issues'. Fortunately for Britain, the Service chiefs of the Second World War quickly learned that the scientifically trained mind had much more to contribute than 'help on details'.

[1] C. H. Waddington, *OR in World War 2: Operational Research Against the U-Boat*, Elek, 1973, p. 247.

6. *Do ensure the venture has a natural leader*—a man with confidence in the venture and the will to drive it to success. The Sappho project leaves no doubt about the importance of the 'business innovator' in successful ventures. But beware of the cult of personality; of a project becoming so clearly identified with one influential person or faction that any objective assessment of the venture's progress is impaired. Lord Robens relates in his autobiography how he rejected an idea to call a new coal-cutting system Automated Longwall Face (ALF), 'knowing it wouldn't be long before it became known as Alf's Face'. He omitted to add that an earlier robot coal-cutting scheme of the National Coal Board, called the Collins Miner, named after the then Board member for production, Harry Collins, had been expensively prolonged long after the commercial logic of the venture had crumbled.

7. *Do see that the venture has all the management skills it requires*—not just scientific and technical enthusiasm but financial, manufacturing, marketing, even labour relations skills commensurate with the task and its targets, and any major changes a successful venture would bring in its wake.

8. *Do think through the financial consequences*—right through to the market place and beyond. As Maddock has shown so graphically, forbidding as the R & D bill can be in a type of activity to which there is no end, no plateau in development costs, the costs that follow can be far more deterring.

9. *Do plan your demonstration or prototype with care*—making sure that it is designed not as an end in itself but to throw up the problems you can expect in the full-scale venture. A prototype that performs perfectly serves no real purpose if it leaves unresolved the problems of the commercial system. Britain paid dearly for the successful performance of an AGR prototype costing only £9 million. The real prototypes turned out to be five commercial AGR power stations costing £1,000 million.

10. *Do be prepared to spend to explore an idea*—even an idea that competes with something you are already backing. A few thousand pounds spent on demonstrating whether an idea is sound can be quicker and cheaper—and far more encouraging—than a painstaking inquiry into the pros and cons.

In an activity fraught with far more pitfalls than any steeplechase I cannot say that observance of these ten rules will guarantee you success. I can say confidently, however, that if you want commercial success in high technology you will ignore at your peril any one of these rules.

Name Index

Subject Index